THE $\mathcal{S}$eed HANDBOOK

Knowledge
Exploitation Fund

Cronfa Datblygu
Gwybodaeth
1 2 NOV 2002

www.seedfusion.com

Two trees will be planted for every one used in the production of this book

THE Seed HANDBOOK

the *feminine* way to create business

Lynne Franks

Thorsons

Thorsons
An Imprint of HarperCollins*Publishers*
77-85 Fulham Palace Road,
Hammersmith, London W6 8JB

The Thorsons website address is:
www.thorsons.com

First published 2000

10 9 8 7 6 5 4 3

© Seed International 2000
Illustrations©Ann Field 2000

Lynne Franks asserts the moral right to be identified
as the author of this work.

A catalogue record for this book is available from the British Library

ISBN 0 7225 3945 2

ILLUSTRATED BY ANN FIELD
DESIGNED BY P*h*.D

Printed and bound in Scotland by Scotprint

ACKNOWLEDGMENTS AND DEDICATION

There has been an incredible network of people who have worked with me in creating SEED, as well as many others who have shown their support in so many ways.

I would like to firstly thank Jenny Daisley, the cofounder of Springboard, the British women's personal development and training company.

Jenny was an integral part of the early development of The SEED Handbook, *co-writing the book's initial outline and contributing the word Dynamics for the D of SEED. Her support and enthusiasm helped me tremendously in the days of my own SEED process to empowerment.*

Jenny, together with her partner, Liz Willis, and the other members of the Springboard team, have empowered thousands of women, particularly in the Third World, and I consider it an honor to have worked with her.

SEED and Springboard share a joint passion for the empowerment of women through economic independence, based on spiritual and values-led principles.

I would also like to thank my illustrator, Ann Field, who has been a constant and graceful companion on my SEED journey. Her intuitive talent and lively paintings have brought SEED to life.

She also brought her talented husband, Clive Piercy, and his design company, Ph.D, into the project, who designed this delightful-looking book so beautifully.

Clive introduced me to Ann Enkoji, the wonderwoman, who helped me pull so much of SEED together, through her research, contacts, and general common sense.

I would like to thank the universe for my two publishers, Joel Fotinos at Jeremy Tarcher/Penguin in the United States, and Eileen Campbell of Thorsons/Harper Collins in the U.K. In my opinion, they and their teams are the best publishers that I could have ever asked for.

They have both constantly supported me throughout my journey. It shows much for their uniqueness that they were able to produce and print this book together in a collaborative harmony that really was a win-win situation.

I would like to thank the wonderful Hazel Henderson for writing the foreword as well as for her constant help and advice, together with all the other folks credited throughout the book who have been so generous with their time and input.

I would like to thank Jeremy Tarcher for the inspiring time I spent with him and his introduction to Laura Golden Bellotti, my editor, who has been a golden delight to work with and just "gets it."

I would like to thank all my close friends and family who encouraged me ceaselessly to write SEED—particularly Gabrielle Roth, who so generously introduced me to Joel Fotinos, now both our American publisher; Denise Linn, who gave me so much good advice in the early, scary days of writing; Kathy Eldon for always being full of good advice; my son-in-law, Jamie Catto, whose intelligent view of SEED gave me a kick-start when I needed it; my assistant, Stephanie Boyd, whose calming influence and dedication contributed so much to the research; Susie Lindsay, for helping me with the U.K. research as well as organizing the many other aspects of my London life, and Joy Young, for all her assistance in the early SEED days before she returned to Oz; Candice Furman, the San Francisco–based super agent, who gave me such great advice, including representing myself; Dee Nolan, Editor of You magazine, for her encouragement and for telling me of some great sustainable case-histories; my colleagues at Globalfusion—Coralie, Dana L., Dayna C., Catherine and Ami—for their constant support as well as allowing me to use them as research material; my lawyer Carol Goodman for some great advice; Dadi Janki and the Brahma Kumaris for their constant support and inspiration on the subject of service and meditation; Bibi Russell and Sayeeda Rahman for their inspiring examples; my sister Sue, for allowing me to pick her brains and help me with the Canadian research; and my friend Michael Kram, for allowing his "funky" paradise home to be turned into the SEED hatching ground, where he would work on his organic garden outside, growing delicious vegetables to feed me, while I was on my computer inside, creating my SEED garden.

And finally, I would like to give thanks to the greatest Creator of all, whose presence I have felt nurturing me throughout this project, since the original planting of the seeds.

I would like to dedicate this book, firstly to my parents my late father, Leslie, who taught me so much about being an entrepreneur and whose energy I felt with me during the writing of the Handbook; my mother, Angela, who worked in partnership alongside of him, taking on all the responsibility so effectively after he became sick and who never ceases to be my mentor, adviser, and friend; my late grandmother Dora, who was the feisty, early entrepreneur in my life; my children, Josh and Jess, whom I'm so proud of and who are SEEDpreneurs of the future; and all the wonderful SEEDpreneurs who never cease to inspire me.

Contents

Seed MANIFESTO

I, ... , *affirm that I will*

Constantly plant seeds as well as pick the blooms

Make the space and time to stay in tune with my higher self

Never let go of the big vision

Put my values, including integrity, compassion, and love at the center of my enterprise

Remember the three R's: respect for self, respect for others,
responsibility for all my actions

Believe in myself so others will, too

Keep humor and laughter as vital ingredients of my business plan

Get up early in the morning

Not neglect my personal relationships, loved ones, and friends in any way

Manifest abundance in all areas of my life

Keep my clutter to a minimum

Recognize my gifts and delegate the rest

Look at difficult situations from all perspectives

Welcome in mentors and mentor others in return

Light candles every day and surround myself with fresh flowers

Give people more than they expect

Talk slowly but think quickly

When I lose, don't lose the lesson

Know my industry

Keep improving my technology skills

Smile when picking up the phone

Remember my body is my most important tool— stretch, exercise,
breathe, go for a walk, dance

Every day try and read a poem, listen to an inspiring piece of music,
look at a wonderful painting or go into nature

Drink six to eight glasses of pure water every day

Listen as well as talk

Learn the rules, and then break some

Know there is nothing more sexy than confidence

Remember that no-one, not even myself is perfect,
but I'm doing the best I can

SIGNED.. *Date*........................

FOREWORD HAZEL HENDERSON

Like Lynne Franks, I, too, started my business on my kitchen table—thirty years ago. I envisioned a world where love would be empowered and where economic textbooks would take account of all the loving, caring sharing, and volunteer work, which is unpaid and unrecognized. I knew I couldn't immediately start a business around my vision—and I also knew that I would be unemployable in most traditional companies. I worked at lots of low-wage jobs, selling women's clothes, at hotel reception and cashiering, as an airline ticket agent, and in a bank and a travel agency. None gave me much sense of meaning or satisfaction.

So I invented my own home-based job—to fit in with raising my daughter and my concern for our health in the polluted environment of New York City. I learned everything I could about the city's pollution and in 1964, I started a citizens' group and began writing and speaking out. I found an advertising agency which volunteered to help us—and then I persuaded the TV and radio stations to broadcast New York City's air pollution index on weather programs. By 1968, my first article had been published in the *Harvard Business Review* on the social responsibilities of business.

Five books and hundreds of speeches and articles later, I am still working at home and love it. I am one of some 20 million home-based "knowledge workers" and my book royalties and lecture fees come from all over the world. I feel very blessed to be able to work at my passion.

I was very lucky in being born into a family in Britain that could afford to care for me. I attended very good little schools that taught me to love reading and writing. I learned about the power of what I later termed "The Love Economy" from my mother. She always had time for all four of her children—in spite of lots of housework, growing all our vegetables and fruits in our garden, and serving as a community volunteer at the local "Meals on Wheels" and the clinic for infants. She was an enterprising woman!

I have known Lynne Franks for many years and I love her spirit, energy, and style. I also respect her business genius and admire her commitment to her higher self, spiritual development, and a healthier, safer, more just world for our children. Like Lynne's children, mine are grown now and my nine-year-old grandson always asks me what I am doing to save the animals that are endangered by human exploitation.

Because you are reading this, I know that you care about all of these issues relating to our common future as much as Lynne Franks and I do. The SEED Handbook will help you manifest your highest visions for your life's purpose and bring your unique gifts and talents into the service of others. By following your purpose and with the SEED roadmap and network you can find the energy to create a wonderful business—however small or large—and have fun doing it.

I will be cheering you on.

Hazel Henderson, AUTHOR
Building a Win-Win World
Anastasia Island
St. Augustine, Florida

INTRODUCTION

There is a revolution going on in the world and it's coming from the grass roots. It's the revolution of the sustainable entrepreneurs, mainly women, and it's about personal growth as well as an economic tool. It's political with a small *p* and it's organic, not structured. It's about creating value, developing relationships, and being financially empowered.

It's the feminine way to create business.

So welcome to *The SEED Handbook*. As you become involved in this unique book, you'll be invited to share the experiences of women who have created their own enterprise and be taken through the steps of the SEED program, which will prepare you to start your own business the feminine way.

I started what became the U.K.'s leading public relations consultancy when I was twenty-one, working from my kitchen table. In the thirty years since then, I have met and spoken with women entrepreneurs from all over the world and from vastly different cultures and backgrounds.

I have observed their courage and vision in starting their own businesses, often in difficult situations, and seen them empower themselves and their families through financial independence.

I have seen the disillusion of many Western women and men with the corporate world and a wish for a quality of life that reflects their inner values.

I've observed a desire to return to community, whether in business or in people's personal lives; the importance of networking; barter re-emerging at many different levels; and the geographic freedom that the new technology is giving us. I've also experienced my own change of lifestyle alongside the emergence of this major shift in society.

After selling my P.R. business at the beginning of the nineties, I spearheaded the launch of the U.K.'s first women's radio station. I subsequently created the What Women Want Festival in London featuring Sinead O'Connor, Chrissie Hynde, and Germaine Greer prior to attending the United Nation's Women's Conference in Bejing. These three events gave me many insights into what I started to see as the beginning of the twenty-first century's feminization of society.

I, like so many others, see a return to spiritual values and the desire of the individual to serve society rather than exploit it. It is a necessary counter-balance to the power of corrupt governments, greedy corporations, the continuance of racial genocide all over the world, and the damage we humans already have done to the environment.

Entrepreneurship is one area where women are leading the way to a new kind of future, where they have more control of their lives and the lives of their children by running healthy businesses to gain economic independence.

FACTS AND FIGURES

Women-Owned Businesses Topped 9 Million in the United States in 1999. This has doubled during the past twelve years, according to a report by the National Foundation of Women. Today there are 9.1 million women-owned businesses in the United States representing thirty-eight percent of all businesses, employing 27.5 million people and generating over $3.6 trillion in sales annually. Many of these women are from the ethnic minorities.

United Nations reports the percentage of women economically active varies widely, from a high of fifty-six to fifty-eight percent in Eastern and Central Asia and Eastern Europe to a low 21 percent in Northern Africa.

Across the world, women-owned firms typically comprise between one quarter and one third of the business population, although this is growing rapidly.

I believe many of these women are running their businesses in a lateral, more open way than the traditional patriarchal style of doing business. Some are creating businesses that are consciously ethical and responsible, while others are just naturally trying to run businesses based on integrity and love.

I believe many more of us out there would like to start a sustainable enterprise but are too scared to take the plunge. Lack of confidence and social conditioning are often the main blockages for many of us starting up. Unfortunately most of us who are urban-dwellers don't live in supportive communities or have access to experienced mentors.

We often feel powerless to take on responsibility for our own lives and change the conditions that make us unhappy, whether it means leaving our high-powered corporate job or going back to work after raising a family. We think we are too old, too young, too nonentrepreneurial, too uneducated, and so on.

That is why we have to hear each other's stories, support and mentor those around us, connect and network, and show each other how to get in touch with the goddess inside, who by planting the seeds can create the sustainable "garden" we want to have in our lives.

I've created SEED so that I can share the experiences I've had and the stories I've heard with you—and so that I can take you through the process of creating the business of your dreams. You'll become a member of the SEED community while reading this book and engaging in the simple exercises designed to focus your energies and to empower you.

WHY SEED?

Preparing to start a business is like planting a garden. We have to nurture seeds—or ideas—while they germinate and we need to know what to do to allow them to bloom into a healthy plant—or enterprise. Starting your own business should be organic, something that grows naturally from who you are as a person. It's about taking responsibility for your own life—and thoroughly enjoying the results.

SEED IS AN ACRONYM FOR SUSTAINABLE ENTERPRISE AND EMPOWERMENT DYNAMICS

In *The SEED Handbook* you will hear the stories of women from around the world who started their own businesses for all kinds of reasons, but who came to the same conclusion —being in charge of your own enterprise is an opportunity to create new ideas and positive change.

The SEED Handbook will show you how to plan a new business based on integrity, personal values, and openness.

The ten-stage SEED program contains practical as well as meditative exercises to give you the confidence to trust your abilities, passions, and values, which will then enable you to create a sustainable enterprise the feminine way.

So welcome to your revolution!

HOW TO USE THE HANDBOOK

Turn back to the SEED Manifesto to start you on your way. Read it through out loud and sign it. You can cut it out and put it where you'll see it every day or leave it in the Handbook to refer to and remind you.

The way to get the most out of this book is to read it through once, taking in the information it contains, and then go through it more slowly, completing the exercises in your own time. It's hard to generalize, but most enterprises should take about a year from the idea germinating until you're ready to launch in full bloom.

Take your time and get it right. The first topic we will be working on is time and space— make sure you've got enough of both to give your enterprise the space to grow.

The Handbook is, unusually, being simultaneously published throughout the English-speaking world, which is why the spelling is in colloquial American English, for which I apologize to my fellow Brits. This is what happens in a global society.

Meanwhile, enjoy and get gardening . . .

chapter 1.

Clearing the ground

Where you create the space and stretch your time to enable you to see your vision.

Before any garden can be seeded, the ground has to be prepared. The rocks and weeds need clearing, the earth has to be turned and the nutrients introduced.

Starting a business is the same way. You have to clear the clutter from your life, internally and externally. You have to create the right environment to be able to grow your vision.

You're about to make some major decisions that could affect the rest of your life. But until you've created some clean space, pulled those weeds, and removed those rocks, you'll never really find the clarity of mind and focus that you'll need to move forward.

For many of us, space and time are probably two of the hardest qualities to find in our busy twenty-first century lives. That's why we're going to start off our SEED mentoring program in this first chapter with stories and exercises to help you stretch time and clear the necessary physical and mental space in which to develop your ideas.

My own natural state is chaos, with millions of ideas and thoughts racing round my head. That's all very healthy during the creative process. But before I start a new project I find it crucial to clear away as much of the internal and external clutter in my life as I can.

Your Desk Area.

You'll need physical space for your SEED work: a place for a desk, or table, files, bookshelves, and so on. But with so much excess "stuff" in every corner of your living environment, how do you begin to create a peaceful yet stimulating physical space?

Clutter can come in many shapes and forms, and it's amazing how easy it is to accumulate old circulars, last year's Christmas cards, and magazines you've already read. Often "preparing the ground" is simply a matter of dealing with these bits of paper that we put

18.

aside because we're sure they are to be important one day. Why not go through all your old files, letters, and junk mail right now and throw away everything that you know you'll never look at again?

Then, organize what's left. Put papers into identifiable files (I always use brightly colored ones, as they encourage me to be organized). Put all your owner's manuals together—I've lost some important ones in the past—and be ruthless with the magazine and newspaper references you've been collecting for years. Spend an evening going through all those old press cuttings and throw out the ones you've no use for. Carefully file away only those articles that you may actually need as references for your proposed enterprise.

Sort out your financial paperwork, too. Put pending bills in an accessible place, and file away your old check books and bank statements. Now that you're thinking of becoming self-employed, start getting used to organizing your receipts and bills in an orderly way.

I'm sure you're getting the picture—start with a grand sweep of all the paper clutter you'll never need again—giving a thought to the poor trees that are sacrificed to give us this overload of documents and information.

19.

Then start with your books. The shelves they're taking up space on will be needed for your new enterprise, and besides, clearing away obsolete materials is very cleansing for the mind.

But what good does it do to straighten out your files and bookshelves when you have no quiet place to call your own? How can you focus on a vision of your new enterprise when you've got young children or noisy teenagers invading your space?

It's important, however small a home you may have, for your family or housemates to support you in keeping a clear area for yourself.

If you have got a large enough home, dedicate one room to your SEED vision. It's so important to create a living, vital space that reflects your energy. We're like plants. We need good space, light, plenty of water, and fresh air. And if you have a window with a view, make sure you can see out when you're working. We need the appropriate environment where we can grow mentally, physically, and spiritually. More on this later, when we'll talk about the Chinese principle of "feng shui." But first, on to more decluttering.

Your Clothes Closet.

And then, of course, there's that delicate area — your wardrobe.

You might ask, "What does cleaning out my closet have to do with starting a new business?" Quite a lot, actually. It's all part of the process of clearing out and getting rid of superfluous "things" you don't need in your life any more. It mentally gives you space to let in all the exciting, new challenges that are coming your way.

Fashion is fashion, and clothes date. Also, if you're planning to leave the corporate world, why do you want to hang on to all those mannish, tailored suits? The new, empowered independent "you" may need to change your image to suit your new lifestyle.

A new hairstyle, natural makeup, and a more relaxed style of dressing can do wonders for your self-esteem. And think how much extra storage space you'll have!

20.

Your Body.

A good spring cleaning, whatever time of the year, is healthy both mentally and physically. Healthy body, healthy mind—and you're going to need all your mental faculties to be in top form once you get going. I'm not talking about some drastic diet, but what about cutting out the junk food? Try and get into a routine of eating regularly and healthily.

I cut out wheat a year ago and after controlling my urges to nibble lots of bread during business lunches, I felt so much better. I found out I was allergic to it, like so many these days, and without wheat in my life I lightened up on every level. I lost weight, but mostly I had more energy. I realized that wheat—bread and pasta, I'm afraid—had made me feel more sluggish for years.

I also stopped drinking coffee and tea years ago. I try and drink lots of pure water every day or herbal tea and find I'm much clearer. Of course, each body is different, so start taking

a note of what you consume each day and try to cut out the things you think may be slowing you down.

The important thing to remember is no excess—whatever your weakness!

Clutter Stories.

Clutter is different in everybody's life, and I got some interesting answers when I started asking friends and colleagues what they consider "clutter."

One said all her clutter is in the trunk of her car. She described it as a "graveyard" of unnecessary material she collects at business meetings and carries around with her until she's going on a trip and needs the space for luggage.

Another friend said her answering machine collects an endless clutter of messages from casual acquaintances calling for free marketing and P.R. advice. She deals with it by calling back when she hopes they're out and leaving a brief message saying she's crazily busy right now and hopes their problems are resolved. Like many I spoke to, and despite her obliging personality, she tries to screen her calls in the evening so she gets some respite.

Laura, my book editor, told me how she throws away all her junk mail directly from her mailbox and doesn't even bring it into her home.

I'm sure all of us have handbags, wallets, and makeup bags that would benefit from a good clear out. I am always pleasantly surprised at the phone numbers, cash, and receipts that I find in the bottom of my bag. I used to have huge handbags but theorized that if I keep the bags small, I won't mislay so many important bits of paper. These days I try and clear out weekly.

Phone numbers on small bits of paper featured in a lot of clutter stories I collected. I tend to transfer mine to an electronic organizer these days, which can be a disaster if accidentally wiped without a backup—I learned my lesson the hard way!

Start putting together a database, either on your computer or manually, with all your contact phone numbers and addresses in alphabetic order as well as with a subject reference. For example, Angela goes under A as a friend, but you should also note that she works in a bank and will be a good person to get advice from when you're ready to open a business account.

The earlier you can start putting together a database, the better. It's always been my experience that this is one job, once you get busy, which is inevitably left to some undetermined time in the future.

I also heard lots of clutter stories about junk we tend to hoard on our computer. Dump those old e-mails, letters, and thoughts that you'll never need again in the trash can. Clean up your virtual desktop in the same way that you clean up your physical desk and see how much clearer your head feels.

Feng Shui at Work.

The Chinese principle of feng shui, where your exterior environment reflects the positive energy you wish to attract in the different areas of your life, is used religiously by Asian businesses. I've had my homes and offices feng-shui'd for years, and I've always found it a highly effective way of redirecting the energy I need.

Feng shui practitioners believe that every object that surrounds you is an external metaphor for your life and affects your psyche. It is an art and science of living in harmony with your environment almost like psychic interior design.

By repositioning furniture, hanging crystals and mirrors appropriately to redirect energy, and using fountains and wind chimes, I believe you can really change your home or your office. Combine this with a powerful intention to heal the negative areas of your life and feng shui can have a very dynamic effect.

When L.A.–based feng-shui experts Herb and Elaine Wright came to my office and home loft, they immediately suggested that I get rid of the dead plants and even my dried rose petals.

I hadn't even noticed the plants had died, but they told me that anything dead and dying can affect us on an unconscious level. We need to have vital, living things around us. Of course, it's all perfect common sense when you think about it.

In fact, everything the Wrights told me improved my home office aesthetically as well as energetically. I already had small fountains in my home, knowing that apart from the soothing effect of the sound of the flowing water, the imagery is a potent symbol for your business and life flowing, rather than stagnating.

I even painted the front door bright red instead of the beautiful blue it was before. Elaine Wright insisted it would bring in good financial fortune, and my colleagues said it made the office seem much warmer.

Every object you place on your desk is a powerful metaphor. I have a small fountain with running water made of rocks and slate on my desk, plus some Chinese Lucky bamboo to attract good fortune, a couple of crystals, and pictures of my kids and loved ones. Other than that it's my computer, some files, and my working papers. A mixture of the practical with some more personally significant objects.

A busy desk is always going to be somewhat cluttered, but try and clear away the non-essentials every night. My kitchen table, where I hold my meetings and work when I'm not on the computer, can end up with a variety of piles of documents. (By the way, warn everyone in your household never to touch your piles of paper—what seems like a mess to anyone trying to clean up usually makes perfect sense to us.)

I do ensure that I clear it up at least twice a day. I also always like to light a candle on the table in the morning as a symbol of positive energy, which I put out when I finish work for the day.

Writer, teacher, and friend Denise Linn has been teaching the importance of what she calls "sacred space" for many years. She told me that it is essential that we create an oasis of sanctuary not only in our homes but in our offices, too. This way we will have the space to hear our inner voice and intuition while we are working in the outside world, and get the most out of all our talents.

Keep my Clutter

TO A MINIMUM

Your Inner Space.

Creating a well-balanced workspace is not the only part of the SEED preparation. You need to create a special place where you can go inside, too, an internal space where you can go to hear your intuitive voice give you guidance with no distractions from the outside world.

Whether you prefer to think that you are listening to your inner voice, your higher self, your intuition, or a divine energy, the fact is that you often have the answers to your questions already in your unconscious.

It's just that we are so bombarded with media, information, noise, and distraction from every side, we often find it hard to hear our own internal voices.

Learning to routinely clear away the "noise" in your life is a crucial aspect of preparing the ground for your new venture. The following exercise will help you to create the quiet you need.

Finding quiet time must become an essential part of your daily routine if you want to succeed. Once you've got your altar ready, it's time to go inside for the first SEED meditation. If you

EXERCISE: SEED QUIET TIME AND MEDITATION

Find a quiet spot, in your garden or a nearby park, surrounded by plants and flowers. Make this your special SEED silence spot. When the climate or circumstances keep you indoors, your place of quiet can be your SEED altar.

Creating your SEED altar can be even more fun than getting your desk organized. Set up a small table against a wall in a quiet space in your home, out of eyesight of your desk. Cover the table with a beautiful piece of cloth and place special objects and pictures representing your dreams and loved ones on it.

Plant some seeds representing your business in a small pot and also place it on your altar. Always have fresh flowers nearby. Nurture the altar, attending to your special objects with care. Have a candle and sweet-smelling incense on it, ready to light. This is your private space, where if you can only spend ten minutes at the beginning and end of the day, your dreams can germinate and start to grow.

haven't meditated before, don't worry that there is some great mystery to it that you won't be able to fathom. I was once told by a wise old Tibetan lama to think of meditation as just the pause between breaths.

Take the time to hear your inner voice, develop your insights, and connect with your true vision. Learn to trust your intuition and strengthen your higher self. Trust it now.

Seed Meditation.

Ask the divine power of the universe to co-create your SEED dream with you and make it real. Imagine you are planting the seeds of your future, and in the silence that you allow yourself, let them gather strength. Leave your mind free and just note the thoughts as they drift through. Trust that your unconscious mind is working at the deepest level to give you the tools you need to bring your garden to life.

Starting an entrepreneurial business is first of all about an idea, a passion that comes from the heart, not the head.

That idea, plus confidence in your own abilities, luck, good judgment, and a lot of hard work, can blossom into a successful enterprise.

But first you have to find the time and space to recognize your needs and your talents, and to learn to hear your own inner wisdom.

Stretching Time.

Even when you have created the appropriate internal and external space, with the constant intrusion of life's obligations and interruptions, preparing the ground for the business you envision won't be possible unless you find a way to stretch time.

Whether you are single or have a family, are currently working nine-to-five or juggling several part-time jobs, something's got to give if you want to devote some quality time to your venture.

Here are some wise words from different women I asked, who've learned to get more out of every hour, without sacrificing their need for relaxation—because starting a business the feminine way involves decreasing your level of stress, not adding to it.

I realized that if I made a very simple change in my day-to-day life, I would have the time I needed to begin to realize my dream. I simply set my alarm clock for one hour earlier. I gave myself an hour every day—as a gift. It's the perfect time for me, too. The rest of the world is quiet and I can think about my project with a fresh mind, before the onslaught of kids and work and routine.

So-called "vampire" friends who just want to suck my energy have had to go now that I'm working for myself. I love seeing my close friends but I don't want to see complainers and professional "victims." The trouble is they are often attracted to strong people and although I'm sympathetic, I want to conserve my energy.

28.

> *For me, carving out the time I needed meant, first of all, noticing where all my "free" time was being eaten up; dinners and movies with friends, phone calls, and watching TV. I had rationalized that I needed the R & R time after work to get together with friends or come home and veg out in front of the tube. But not every single night of the week! Now I keep the date with myself to work on my business plan two nights a week.*

> *I make lists of everything I have to do the night before. I write them in an attractive notebook and stretch time by crossing out the jobs that aren't really that important—the time they would have taken up now belongs to my SEED project.*

I talked to lots of high-achievers, some with small children, about how they stretch time and fit everything they need to into their lives. Of course, successful earners rely on a support system of childcare, cleaning help, and so on. However, everyone agreed that it was by keeping some space for themselves, just a few minutes here and there, that helped them to have the clarity and time to do their work. Panicking definitely didn't help anyone.

Walks around the block, regular food and restroom breaks, lots of lists, five minutes' silence now and then, making verbal lists into handheld recorders when stuck in traffic, making your phone calls first thing in the morning, and definitely remembering to breathe seem to work for most.

Of course, in these days of technology we have our mobile phones with us. I rarely give my number out, as I would hate it ringing all the time, but at least I can make the calls I need to when I'm travelling.

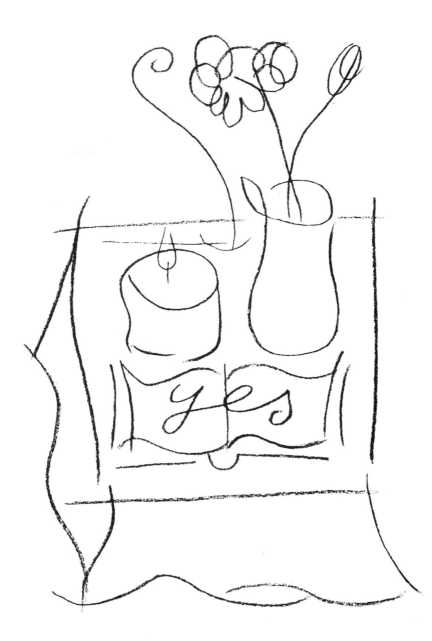

MEDITATION: GROUNDING YOURSELF FOR YOUR FUTURE

So now that we have cleared some space for your dreams to grow, it's time to ground yourself in front of your special SEED quiet place or altar. As a fitting end to this first SEED chapter, meditate with our special prayer of gratitude, aloud or silently:

"I give thanks to the gods of my special garden for empowering me with the strength and clarity to nurture my seeds and bring them to full growth. I ask for my higher self to join me in courageously moving into my future."

Where we examine
your courage and
confidence and
face your fears.

Planting
the
Roots
of your Courage

How confident and courageous are you? Do you feel ready to create your own garden or are you quite understandably frightened about the prospect of achieving your potential and becoming a SEED entrepreneur?

It takes great courage to be true to yourself, but that's what you need to start a sustainable enterprise based on values and ethics. It takes courage to behave honorably, even with your back against the wall. But if you have that courage you will always succeed.

You'd be surprised how much courage you are already using in daily life and don't give yourself credit for. Just getting up in the morning and dealing with your day can take an enormous amount. Look back at your day today and list at least five things you did that took a lot of courage. Sitting in the dentist chair for three hours having needles stuck in my mouth and then going out to face L.A. traffic were definitely two of mine.

34.

The truth is, we can do anything we want—it's our own doubts and lack of self-confidence that hold us back. And, according to my friend singer/songwriter Celina, there is nothing more sexy than confidence!

What Are We So Afraid Of?

Before you can cultivate the soil for your new enterprise, using the courage it's going to take to get started, you'll need to face up to any lurking fears that may be inhibiting you.

What are some common fears that many of us share? Do you fear public speaking or putting yourself in the limelight? A young music-writer friend said she loves to perform but hates being "seen." Her five years as a college DJ were under a pseudonym, and she fell out with her family over her nephew's bar mitzvah when she was too shy to make a speech. Now she works in a job in promotions where she has to be up front. Having faced her fears, she is enjoying every minute of it.

Standing up and being seen is often a big fear for many of us. And sometimes we end up doing the very things that bring up our fears. I felt very self-conscious about being "seen," too, and yet always seem to be in the public eye.

I was making speeches in front of hundreds, sometimes thousands, of people and regularly appearing on TV programs. I would go into a cold sweat for at least an hour before and have to run to the bathroom regularly.

The way I got over my fears was to start asking my higher self for help beforehand. I heard my inner voice remind me to just speak from the heart. I knew my subject after all, and audiences always respond to honest, heartfelt talks—something politicians should try and remember!

Confrontation is also a big fear for many, particularly women. It's always so much easier to say yes or just put off those difficult moments. I certainly hate it. But running your own business is full of those times when you have to face uncomfortable situations with others.

What I've learned, albeit slowly, is that the longer you put off confrontation, the harder it is. It is always better to express how you feel, whether in personal or professional relationships. What we have to learn is that confrontation may be uncomfortable, but if we stay true to ourselves and come from a place of grace, rather than anger, it doesn't have to be unpleasant. That's the "Feminine Way."

My very feminine lawyer, San Francisco–based Carol Goodman, specializes in what she calls "Positive Dispute Resolution." She explained to me that the word confrontation brings up images of angry people. "There is a tendency for a lot of guilt to be present in confrontations, which makes people either overcompensate or get aggressive. It's human nature, during uncomfortable situations, for each party to want to be right and to prove the other wrong."

"However, it's far better to try and look at the situation as an objective outsider. There will invariably be extra factors that you don't know about that are influencing the other person. You should never look on confrontation as a battle, but an opportunity to understand how each other is feeling. Learn to dialogue to keep options open for the future and try and see the situation as the other person sees it. It is never about winning and losing but to learn by the experience and move forward in a positive way."

35.

How Does Courage Grow? Success Stories.

A large percentage of the hundreds of young women and a few young men that I trained over the years in the P.R. agency have started their own businesses.

Before I interviewed the many, diverse entrepreneurs, mainly women who make up the majority of the case histories in the Handbook, I decided to research my own former employees to see what had motivated them and given them the courage to start their own enterprise.

I had the great fortune to work with some very exceptional people in my days of running Lynne Franks P.R., and I knew their stories would inspire others.

I contacted many of them to ask them what gave them the confidence to become entrepreneurs themselves. They all told me, somewhat to my surprise, that I'd asked them to do the impossible and empowered them by trusting them to get on and do it.

36.

They reminded me that I'd ask them to get a story on a client on the front page of a national newspaper or organize a graffiti art exhibition for Swatch watches in a central London venue within a month. I always asked them to do things that I knew they were capable of, even if they didn't.

Obviously, they reasoned, if they could achieve the impossible for me, they could do it for themselves. I saw their potential and got them to see it, too.

Former shop assistants, art college graduates, and secretaries are now running their own businesses all over the world. One is a top Hollywood agent, another a successful marketing consultant in Melbourne, Australia. Many of them are running P.R. agencies still networked up to each other as friends and a support group.

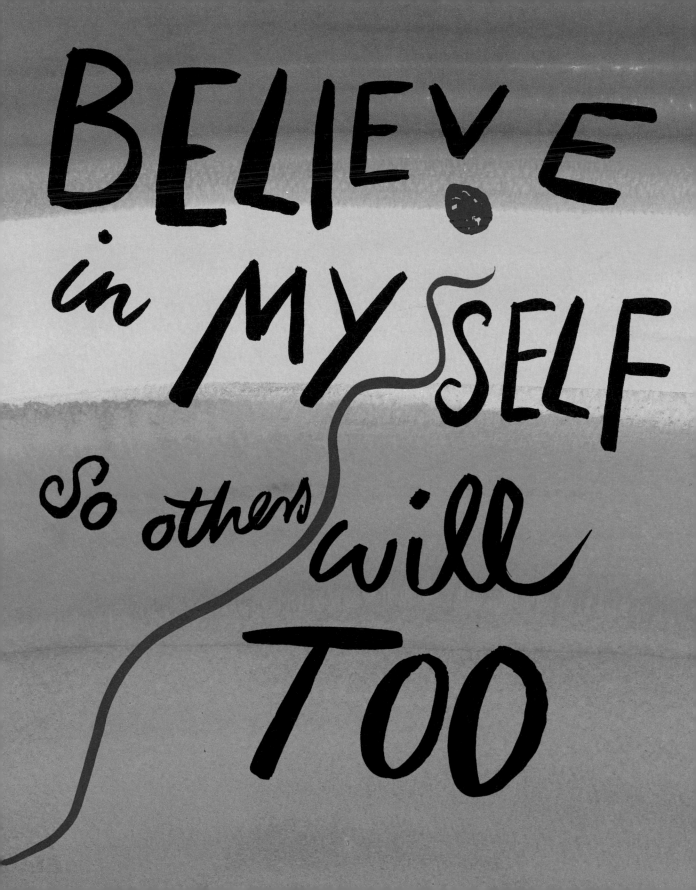

Daniella—Cloning Courage.

Daniella Milton, now running an agency in L.A. representing many of Hollywood's top makeup, hair, and costume-designing talent, reminded me how she'd come to work for me at seventeen with no skills.

"I'd left school at fifteen and been working in a shop. You offered me a job to come and work in the office when I came for a different type of job. You saw something in me that I didn't even see in myself and even though I couldn't use a typewriter, you showed me I could learn office skills."

Daniella reminded me that when she joined the agency in its early days we worked around one large table in our trendy Covent Garden offices. It was by listening to me and other experienced P.R. consultants that she learned the ropes.

"I used to mirror myself on you to the point that I'd be accused of becoming a clone. But that's how I learned to use my own 'people' skills, which help me in my business today. Filmmaking is a very budget-oriented industry and negotiating between movie producers and talent is tough.

The reason I started my own business is that I saw the gap between the back room creatives and the producers. The creatives hate having to talk money, and while I was an assistant to actress Anjelica Huston and on locations in Santa Fe, I offered to help out a costume designer friend negotiate her latest movie."

Because no one else was doing this kind of work, the word got out. People started phoning Daniella up to ask her to represent them. With a young baby and an actor husband, Daniella wasn't in a position to give up work.

"I told Anjelica what was going on and she kindly agreed for me to go part-time, go on half-salary, and start my business while still working for her. I paid to put my own phone line in and started from there."

It was obvious after six months that Daniella needed to focus on her agency full-time, so she moved to a shared office in Hollywood. "My young son is too demanding for me to work at home, plus you have to be in a centrally located office to be taken seriously."

Pregnant with her second child, Daniella invested in a computer, fax, and phones, stationery, business cards, and a launch party. She now represents more than twenty-five talented

38.

movie creatives and has rapidly built up a reputation with some of Hollywood's top producers as a canny negotiator.

"I don't see why business should be unfriendly. I think it's important for any deal to be a win-win situation, and the negotiating skills I learned while working as a P.R. consultant have definitely shown me how to stay strong and confident while seeing situations from all points of view."

Vicky — Thrown in the Deep End.

Vicky Pepys joined my agency in the early eighties from art school full of highly creative ideas but with no business experience. She soon charmed all she met with her no-nonsense, down-to-earth Northern England charm.

Vicky told me that after working for my agency and being asked to do the impossible, anything *was* possible.

"You drove us to believe in ourselves. We learned to be flexible, think on our feet, and bring our skills to the front. We were thrown in at the deep end and learned to turn around whatever life threw back at us."

Vicky now lives in a remote village with her husband, Simon, in rural England. She runs a one-woman P.R. and marketing agency, in between looking after her chickens, writing for the village newspaper, and organizing local community events.

She has set up her consultancy based on three precepts. Firstly, make sure you have a guaranteed income from commercial work; secondly, always leave time for creative work that you love which may not earn you much income; and thirdly, use your skills to help the community.

Vicky has managed to do this perfectly. She works three days a week as marketing consultant for one of the U.K.'s largest manufacturers of cashmere clothing and has more creative flexibility organizing projects such as fashion shows and writing promotional material for cultural events.

As part of her commitment to the community, Vicky also exchanges her services for barter. "I swapped my bicycle for a stone wall when I first came to live here, and I'm quite happy to do bits of writing for local people in return for the odd half sheep for the freezer. At the moment I'm getting stories in the national press for a local farmer about government controls on the price of wool. I'm looking forward to a whole sheep for pulling that off."

Ann-Marie and Harriet—Fearless Ozzies.

Australian-born Anne-Marie Fitzgerald and Harriet Ayre-Smith were senior P.R. executives at my agency at different times before going back home to Oz. They both subsequently started their own public relations and marketing consultancies in their home cities of Melbourne and Sydney, respectively.

Harriet started her own business more recently after several years running the public relations for Chanel in Australia. "I decided to start a business with some trusted friends as partners. I am a single mother with a small daughter and want to feel I have business partners to rely on who can handle my work when I have to be with my daughter."

She, like many others from my agency, says she found the confidence to open her business because I made her feel there was nothing she couldn't do.

"You were a powerful role model who provided an environment that encouraged and supported new talent. You made us work hard but we learned so much. It was a family, yet still exciting and inspiring."

Harriet said laughter is the most common sound in her agency's offices and that the relationships between her and her partners is based as much on humor as it is on professionalism and creativity.

Ann-Marie's agency, Bruize, has built up a reputation across the Pacific Rim for professional, creative work. When she first went home, she worked in a highly paid corporate fashion job but decided she wanted more creative control.

"I got offered some freelance work, I was told I would keep my boss as a client and thought, why not do it for myself?" With the support of her photographer boyfriend, Kerry,

EVERYDAY
TRY AND READ
A POEM, LISTEN
TO AN INSPIRING
PIECE OF MUSIC,
LOOK AT A
WONDERFUL PAINTING
OR GO INTO NATURE

now her business partner and husband, she found a small office, thought of a company name, and printed up her business cards.

"I paid for everything as I went along, computers, equipment, and so on. I never had to borrow from the bank and was, I suppose, quite conservative, putting any profit straight back in the business."

Women are less risk takers, according to Ann-Marie. "We're traditionally the housekeepers and control the budgets. We are naturally more cautious." She also told me that in Australia right now sixty percent of all new small businesses are being started by women. It's the women who have the longevity in small entrepreneurial businesses, too, and Ann-Marie is sure it's because they take less risks.

"I know I could have a bigger business if I want but I'd rather stay a manageable size with quality clients. I want a continuity of clients rather than running around pitching for new ones. I never cold-call but get recommended. My policy is to invest in each client and they in turn stay loyal to us."

The reason I have told the stories of just a few of the many talented individuals who worked for me over the years is not to give myself a pat on the back. It's just to point out that we all have unlimited potential to create our dreams, whether someone else is encouraging you or you are challenging yourself.

> **EXERCISE: DARE YOURSELF TO DO SOMETHING YOU FEAR**
>
> *I'm now going to ask you to do something you've always wanted to do but have never dared. It shouldn't have anything to do with work but should be an activity that you would always regret you never tried. Ideally, you should do it this week, but if your secret dream is to go to India, then at least start making arrangements this week and commit to going.*

It could be parachuting out of a plane, scuba diving, or hot-air ballooning. Or it could be something more gentle but just as difficult for you, like singing a song in front of your friends and family, painting a self-portrait, having a look around a sex shop, or going to a rock 'n' roll concert on your own and dancing all the way through.

Although I've often wanted to, I've always dreaded going to the movies on my own. I always imagined everyone in the audience would be staring at me, thinking I didn't have any friends even though there are those who say going to the movie theater on their own is bliss. They tell me it's the only way they can feel the emotional space to really experience the movie. I, on the other hand, get completely paranoid.

So think of something little and doable that you can do to challenge your fears this week. Maybe it's just phoning up your ex who you never completed with and saying good bye in a loving way. It's never too late for any of us to remove yet more barriers that are blocking us from moving into our full potential.

So, take some time in your SEED quiet space and think deeply about what you've always wanted to do but never dared.

I'VE ALWAYS WANTED TO

_____

AND THIS WEEK

I'M GOING TO DO IT

Once you've taken this big step, you'll see how your self-confidence grows. It will take you giant leaps toward creating your SEED dreams.

PRETEND YOU'RE CONFIDENT, REMEMBER WHAT YOU ALREADY KNOW, AND IDENTIFY THE WISE WOMAN INSIDE.

Denise Linn told me recently how easy it is to fool people that you are confident. "If you act like you have confidence, pretty soon you believe it yourself."

She also reminded me that life doesn't always turn out the way you intend. "We have to remember how small children behave. When they fall over they just pick themselves up and start again."

Unfortunately, too many of us, particularly women, underestimate ourselves. Our self-esteem is needlessly low. This could be blamed on two thousand years or more of a patriarchal society; the advertising, fashion, and beauty industries; or our self-grown sense of inadequacy. Women of my age often feel that they've missed the boat and have given up on achieving their dreams.

But we mature women shouldn't give up so easily. After all, we're the baby boomers who grew up with the freedom of the sixties and now have the knowledge of the wise woman. Our experiences are there to be shared with our sons, daughters, and young friends.

Sharing with others always helps build up confidence, particularly for women. Why don't you join up with some friends with compatible skills and ideas and swap wisdom? You can work on the SEED program together and maybe even start a joint enterprise. Supporting and nurturing each other is the SEED way.

Failing at anything is just another lesson. As I've suggested in the SEED Manifesto, remember, "When I lose, I don't lose the lesson." I've made countless mistakes in my professional life as well as my personal life, but it hasn't stopped me. Far from it.

My self-esteem can still get shaky, though. It got particularly wobbly after splitting up with my husband after twenty years and retiring from the agency I'd founded. For a while I completely lost touch with my sense of self and what I'd achieved.

Then through my spiritual practice and support from loving friends I got back in touch with who the real Lynne Franks is. It wasn't about the outer successes I'd achieved but the love that I gave and received from so many.

I learned to connect with my higher self and through that with God. I would just have to sit out in nature, connect with the beauty surrounding me, and let go of my own ego. My insecurities would drop away and I would remember to start trusting my own flow again.

It may take a little time, but that divine energy is on tap for all of us. Why not take this opportunity to go to your special SEED space in nature or in front of your altar and open yourself up to your natural flow?

46.

AFFIRMATION FOR COURAGE AND CONFIDENCE

Ask the universe for courage to manifest your dream. Take a few minutes of silence to nurture your soul, visualizing yourself watering the soil in your SEED garden. Then repeat an affirmation for courage and confidence.

You can make up your own or use our SEED prayer:

"I am watering my soul with the universal flow. I trust in my higher self and have courage to achieve my potential and realize my dreams."

Repeat this out loud after your twice-daily meditation and see how quickly you come to believe it.

Soul
to
Soil

Where you dig deep inside to
recognize your strengths, weaknesses,
passions, and skills.

What kind of gardener are you? Do you want to nurture your plants from seeds slowly and carefully or let them grow wild? Who are you now and who do you want to be? What are your passions and what are your gifts?

What Puts the Sunshine in Your Soul?

How do you most enjoy yourself, what are your interests and talents, and how do you turn them into a business?

Sometimes your passions can be the most obvious things. What makes you light up inside when you think about doing it? And is there a way to combine this pleasure with your existing professional experience and skills?

I met a young English woman at an event some years ago, which was honoring the Prince's Trust, Prince Charles's organization that encourages young people to set up their own businesses. She published one of the world's top fan magazines while still a teenager, inspired by the Trust and her passionate admiration of Barbara Streisand. How wonderful that she transformed her activities as a fan into an enterprise, which enabled her to enjoy her hobby for a living.

Of course, for many of you, just transferring your professional career from employee status to freelance seems the easiest way to start your own business. But does your current or former job light up your life? And for those of you who aren't currently working—do you want to go back to your last job or training or do you want to move into a totally new career? Is there a way of taking elements of your experience and combining them with more of your personal values and gifts?

Let's look first at how you enjoy spending your time the best—what lights up your soul. Make a list of twenty activities that you currently enjoy doing the most. These can be professional or personal. They could include going for a walk, dancing, going to art galleries, meeting people, or surfing the Internet.

50.

EXERCISE: WHAT ARE YOUR PASSIONS?

MY SOUL LIGHTS UP WHEN I . . .

(LIST TWENTY ACTIVITIES)

....

....

....

....

....

51.

....

....

....

....

....

....

....

....

....

....

Just to make sure we're not overlooking any passions that you've let go of, let's look at your preferred activities and hobbies as a child and a teenager.

For example, when I was a child I was always the organizer of the other neighborhood children's games, and I loved dancing and reading. When I was a teenager, I was still organizing everyone's social activities, dancing, reading, and writing. Now I am an adult and I am still doing the same things. I now appreciate that amongst my gifts are people skills, organizing events, absorbing information, and writing—ideal skills for a person with a career in public relations, journalism, and public speaking, who loves to dance whenever possible.

A friend of mine spent much of her childhood and teen years on the telephone to all her friends advising them on their parent or relationship problems. Needless to say, she grew up to become a psychologist.

Another, now a successful interior designer, told me she used to love making furniture for her toys when she was small, using her mother's sewing machine to make little curtains, and constantly redesigning her bedroom as a teenager.

52.

EXERCISE: REMEMBERING WHAT MY PASSIONS
WERE WHEN I WAS YOUNG

When I was, a child I always played at . . .

....

....

....

....

....

....

When I was, a teenager I used to spend my time . . .

....

....

....

....

....

....

Your Attributes: the Good, the Bad, and the Not So Bad.

Now that you've defined what you really enjoy doing with your time, let's look at your strengths and weaknesses. Once you have honestly assessed your passions, skills, and problem areas, you can then start looking for a picture to emerge of how you can use what you've got and what you love to create a business that can thrive.

Sometimes it's difficult to be very objective about yourself, so after making this list of your strengths and weaknesses check them out with your nearest and dearest as well as your work colleagues. Choose people who you know will tell you the truth.

Of course, one person's strength is another person's weakness—it's just a matter of balance and context.

You may prefer writing to speaking to people and see that as a strength, as one of my friends does. However, even though that does make her a good writer in her job, it also means she is unable to deal with people face-to-face, which is clearly a weakness.

Having a sense of humor in just about any situation is obviously a plus, but not to take situations seriously when they obviously need to be is surely a minus.

What we have to learn to do is either to turn our weaknesses into positives, or even just weed them out. For example, I think too fast sometimes and say things prematurely or finish people's sentences for them—a very irritating quality. That's why one of the messages in the SEED Manifesto is to "think fast but speak slowly." A personal reminder to me that it's important to think on your feet but not blurt it out of your mouth.

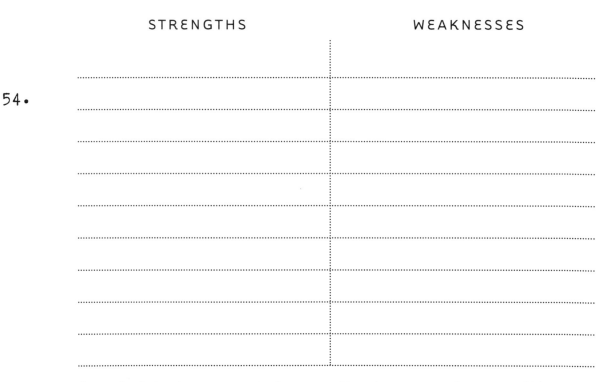

EXERCISE: YOUR PLUSES AND MINUSES

Make a list of your strengths and weaknesses, taking into account not only your self-assessment, but what others have told you as well.

STRENGTHS	WEAKNESSES

54.

As you begin to plan your new business, consider where your weaknesses could become positive attributes. For example, if you are always restless—think of a business that requires a lot of travelling. If you don't like being with adults very much but love children, why not create a business based on childcare or children's education?

Clearly, there are some weaknesses which just have to be accepted and taken into account when you are planning your future. If you don't enjoy crowds, create a business where you don't have to deal with any.

It's all common sense, but it's amazing how we sometimes ignore our essential personality traits and inner qualities when we take on a particular job or plan our working life.

Skills, Resources, Knowledge, and Contacts: Finding Your Inner Entrepreneur.

The next things we need to look at are the professional and personal skills we have that will be of use to us as entrepreneurs, as well as our resources, knowledge, and contacts.

I believe we all have an entrepreneur inside. For example, you need to be an entrepreneur and time management expert if you are a mother and home keeper—juggling the workload, organizing your family's schedules, and overseeing household budgets. You need to be an entrepreneur if you are an artist or a writer. You have to buy your tools, produce your work, and then, most importantly, sell it. Whether you're a corporate executive or a secretary, you organize your work in a creative, entrepreneurial way. We all have the potential skills to have our own business, whether they are currently in use or a bit rusty.

It's easy to forget how much knowledge we have accumulated or learned over the years. Don't take for granted that you've always loved cooking and create great original recipes or have tremendous taste in clothes for yourself and others. Maybe you've been studying natural health for years and have become an expert on nutrition and herbs. What about the art classes at school that you loved but abandoned when you decided to study law?

Gardening, personal finance, nurturing others, good with animals, shopping, do-it-yourself around the home—you'd be astounded by what you are an expert on, and how such skills might translate.

In addition, there are skills that you've picked up during your career that you're probably not even aware of. Office management, interior design, scheduling, budgeting skills, salesmanship, presentation, psychology, marketing, writing—I'm sure the list goes on and on.

EXERCISE: ACKNOWLEDGING YOUR SKILLS, KNOWLEDGE, AND CONTACTS

My skills, both professional and personal, are:

....

....

....

The subjects I know best are:

....

....

....

....

....

56.

My best SEED contacts are:

NAME	CONTACT NUMBERS	HOW SHE/HE CAN HELP

As for contacts, you'd be surprised just how many people you know who could be very useful when you start your own business—and delighted to be so. Ex-bosses and ex-colleagues who may be able to advise you or introduce you to people who can; supportive friends and family; people with money to invest; acquaintances in the media, who might help you to publicize your new business.

Remember that friend of a friend who is a graphic designer and would be happy to design your logo for free or cheap, or an uncle who is a printer and could give you credit on your first marketing materials. Think hard if you know anyone who is, or is married to, a tax expert or a lawyer. They can be very important. Even include your teenage children, whose computer skills could be a tremendous help.

Don't feel guilty thinking you are using people. Just be prepared to help others in return.

Clarifying Your Motives.

While we're digging deep, are you really clear why you want to start a business? If you simply want an easier life, then stop here, because having your own business is not about having it easy.

On the other hand, if you want creative fulfillment, challenges, fun, and the knowledge that you can achieve your potential, together with a tremendous amount of hard work, then read on.

This might be a good opportunity to clarify your thoughts and make a list of all the reasons you think you want to start your own business.

Take some time to think about this and be as honest as you can be. Are you trying to prove something to other people—probably your parents, friends, or partner—or are you creating a business for yourself? Is it to make money or do you want creative fulfillment? Do you crave recognition or just freedom? Do you want a business so that you can contribute to society or so that you can retire early? Or is your motive a combination of all of these?

And think about whether you really want to start your own business or simply want to work on your own as a freelance consultant. One thing can lead to the other, if you want it to. But at least you'll know where to start.

Take the time to clarify your motivation. It will help you later when you decide what kind of business you want. If you crave recognition, for example, you won't mind working in a high-profile enterprise. But if you just want to make enough money to retire early, you may decide to open a business which may not be your burning passion, but will guarantee to make you a lot of money.

In fact, most successful businesswomen I asked said they want financial independence but that money and fame have never been their main motivation. It's been far more about creative fulfillment and a desire to give something back to society.

EXERCISE: DISCOVERING YOUR MOTIVATION

Now it's time to look at your own motivation. Do you want a new challenge in your life? Do you want to work less hard? Do you want to make millions? Do you want a complete change of direction in your career? Do you want to start your own business because you're disillusioned with the conventional corporate world? Whatever the true reasons are, make sure you're aware of them as you plan your future enterprise.

I want to start my own enterprise because . . .

....

....

....

....

....

....

How Does a Business Take Root in Your Soil?

Now that you've examined your motivation, skills and knowledge, strengths, weaknesses, and passions, is a picture starting to emerge of how you can bring them all together to create a business?

For example, I was twenty-one years old when I started my P.R. agency from my kitchen table. I don't remember analyzing why I wanted to start my own business. I knew I wasn't very good at working for other people. I hated being told what to do and I had always had a natural instinct to lead rather than to follow, right from childhood.

Unconsciously though, when I look back over the years, I'm sure I was trying to prove myself to my family. My mother was frustrated that the Second World War had interrupted her career plans to be a journalist, and I wanted to do it for her. My matriarchal grandmother who lived with us was very demanding and my father was a manic depressive, whose attention I wanted to hold.

I didn't have much to lose by starting my own business. I loved networking, fashion, and popular culture and after leaving school when I was sixteen years old, I had worked in advertising and on teenage magazines as a secretary and trainee journalist.

I ended up working in a public relations agency by default in between journalist jobs and realized that I'd found my forte. I could still do the writing I enjoyed, but I was also using other parts of my creative brain, arranging events and dealing with many different types of people. I learned to think on my feet and be proactive, not reactive.

After just three months working for someone else, I rashly decided to start working for myself. I had one client, fashion designer Katharine Hamnett, who was the same age and had also just started her own business.

She offered to pay me twenty pounds (thirty dollars) a week when she could afford it to do her publicity, so with encouragement from my family and boyfriend, I decided to try on my own.

Energy, enthusiasm, and naivety kept me going until I realized after a year or so that I had a proper business and that I'd better start learning how to run one.

Remember that no-one, not even I, am perfect but I'm doing the best I can.

I made lots of mistakes but by sheer perseverance and passion managed to survive and eventually turn the company into a multimillion-dollar P.R. agency with an international reputation. That was then.

This is now. Having decided to write *The SEED Handbook* together with starting Globalfusion, a new communications business, since moving to California from the U.K. when I turned fifty, I was determined to be somewhat more circumspect. I wanted to do things differently this time around. We are living in different times and without losing my entrepreneurial spirit, I wanted to be more conscious and responsible.

I wanted my values to be at the front end of the business, and I wanted to fulfill my vision and game plan. This time around I constantly ask myself why I have started again and make sure I'm still in line with my vision. I'm also far more aware of my strengths and weaknesses. Even after all these years in business, I am still consciously trying to change my old negative patterns that can get me into trouble, such as saying "yes" too quickly instead of "I'll think about it and come back to you."

61.

The Whole Picture.

Whatever business you decide to create, it will not be your whole life, but it will have to fit into your life. What are your personal visions and how do they fit in with having your own business? How and where do you want to live—city, town, or country? Do you have small children? How much time do you want to spend with them? Does it make more sense for you to work at home? To have a balanced life, you have to judge it as a whole, not in separate compartments.

If you had to look at your life a few years down the line, would you still be happy running a business doing the same kind of work you're doing now, or would you want to do something completely different?

Remember, we do write our own life stories.

Putting the Pieces of the Jigsaw Puzzle Together.

62.

You've been doing some very intensive internal research in the course of this chapter and have unearthed a lot of information. Take some time to read your exercise responses several times over in the next few days. Redigest and refine your answers to discover the ones that particularly resonate with your intuition. Select the skills, passions, strengths, and knowledge that you'd really like to include in your enterprise, taking into consideration your weaknesses and motivation. Put the different points together, like pieces of a jigsaw puzzle that make up your perfect enterprise.

Make notes of the words that particularly stand out as you are going to need them to Seed Your Vision in the next chapter. You're starting to design the garden that is going to bring you to the next stage of *The SEED Handbook*, where you will be deciding the type of enterprise you want to create.

MEDITATION: RECOGNIZING YOUR SKILLS AND PASSIONS

Now is the time to ground yourself again with your daily meditation. You need to ask the universe for wisdom to select the right answers that will work together to bring you closer to building your SEED garden.

In front of your SEED altar or in your special SEED place in nature, say the following prayer out loud or internally.

"I give thanks to the universe for letting me dig deeply into my soul to recognize my gifts, skills, and passions that will help me to design my seed garden."

chapter

4

Seed Visioning

Where you start mapping
the qualities and feelings
you want in your business
... and researching reality.

At this point in the SEED program you may feel very sure you know what kind of business you wish to start. Or you may think you have some idea of what you want to do but are not certain. You may even feel absolutely clueless about what type of enterprise you want but just know you want to work for yourself.

Either way, in this chapter we are now going to create the opportunity for you to "feel" into the type of work you want to do. It will give you the chance to confirm that you are on the right path with what you are already thinking of doing, but it may also bring a completely new career idea into your consciousness that fits in far better with your personal values, passions, and skills.

66.

Sometimes, and more often than we've been conditioned to think, it is more fruitful to intuitively "feel" your way into your future than get there by an intellectual process. The SEED way is to "feel" first and then approach those feelings with logical, pragmatic research and analysis. Well, that's the theory anyway—I know that many women entrepreneurs, myself included, let their emotions lead them entirely. But having experienced some rough going as a result of purely emotional decision-making, I do believe it is necessary to combine both methods.

So, as if you were designing your garden, start thinking of all the different plants and flowers you want to include. Let's begin by looking at some of the qualities you'd like to have in your business. Our SEED Visioning process is a simple but effective way to gather our thoughts.

EXERCISE: CREATING YOUR SEED VISION POSTER

Get an 18" x 24" poster board. You are going to be sticking images and words on it today to signify the theme of your enterprise, and you'll be adding to it in the weeks to come.

First, find a photograph of yourself looking happy and place it at the center top of your poster board. Then find an image that represents the greatest gardener of us all, the Universal Creator, and put it in the center.

I find the image of Ceres, the ancient Greek goddess of agriculture, who sows the seeds of abundance to feed us, has inspired me in this project.

If you feel it appropriate to put a picture of your family, particularly if you have children, with you in your vision, then do it now.

Before you go any further, find five or ten minutes to be silent in your special SEED place or in front of your altar. Ask for guidance from the creator, to be in touch with your inner-most thoughts and dreams during the process of this exercise.

Next, you'll need to gather some of the magazines and images that you refused to throw away during your decluttering because you felt they would come in useful one day. If you're so organized that you don't keep any old magazines, buy some new ones or borrow some old ones from friends and family, but warn the current owners that they'll be returned with pictures cut out.

If you've always thought that you were in the accountancy profession but cooking is your private passion, now is the time to get out some beautifully illustrated recipes and delicious pictures of food.

If you've always loved designing interiors, either as a hobby or work, get the architectural or interior magazines you admire in front of you. If animals are your passion, it's time to get out some pictures of your preferred breeds, particularly the ones you like to play with.

Don't look on this as a school assignment—be intuitive and enjoy the process of finding images that inspire you to engage in the work you'd love to do. We're going to have some fun, cutting out our favorite images and starting to make a collage of, as the song goes, "a few of our favorite things."

Your images may include "raindrops on roses or whiskers on kittens" if you're a photography nut, or a picture of your ideal fruitcake recipe, or a wild garden, full of exotic plants. Basically, whatever turns you on.

And we're only starting today. Don't panic. SEED Visioning is an ongoing process—leave yourself plenty of space so you can keep adding images that stand for what you love.

And it's not only pictures and images that are going onto your SEED Vision poster; it's words, too. Look back to the last chapter and the lists you made of your passions, now and when you were younger, together with your gifts and skills.

Which words resonate and jump off the page? Words like "networking," "writing," and "dogs"? Did your lists include phrases like "going shopping," "making money," "being part of a team," or "talking on the telephone"?

Perhaps your preferred skills include computer literacy, budgeting, and time management. And your passion is sculpture or riding horses. Take some plain white paper and thick colored markers and write down the words and phrases to which you feel most connected. Then cut out these words and paste them on your Vision poster. Once they become part of your SEED Vision, you'll start "feeling" the big picture.

Would you want to open a riding stable—you'll need organizational skills as well as a love of horses. Or could your vision be to open an eco-travel agency on the Net, where you have to love being a planet traveller, a good networker, and an extremely proficient budget analyst? (Of course, the last two are pretty essential in starting any business and often don't go hand-in-hand.)

Maybe there are other words and phrases, too, which make you feel good, such as "ocean spray," "travelling continents," "the fragrance of flowers," or "the sound of children play-ing." These could all be clues for your SEED enterprise. Conjure the most meaningful words and images, and put them all on your Vision poster.

When you have completed the first "sweep," place the emerging picture up in a visible spot that you'll pass several times a day. Keep adding to your SEED Vision with images and words as you progress through the Handbook.

And if you feel you have too many images to fit on one poster, make yourself a SEED Vision book, sticking the pictures in a large scrapbook. Do make sure that you refer to it daily, at least once.

Don't forget to include words like "partners" if that's what you're thinking about or "work-ing from home," and see if they "feel" right after a period of time. Follow your instincts and remove any images or words from your Vision poster if you discover that they don't resonate.

Incidentally, the concept of visioning, which I learned from Denise Linn, works just as effectively with relationships, a new home, or even planning your holidays.

68.

Envisioning More Than One Possibility.

The list of possibilities for combining your hobbies, your passions, and your skills into a business are endless if you use your imagination. Within our diverse and changing world of technological developments and return to sustainable values, there is unlimited potential for both innovative and traditional businesses, for new ideas as well as old ones with a new twist.

Why not consider how many types of businesses you could feasibly be interested in, just in case the first doesn't work out? For example, if your passion is making clothes you could consider designing and selling sewing patterns to fabric shops and quilting supply stores or to individual customers through the mail. This could be less of a risk and more enjoyable work than supplying finished garments to shops or individuals.

Or, if you find that there are already too many at-home pre-schools in your area (although there are rarely too many good ones) and you want to work at home with young children, it's time to think about other possibilities. Perhaps you could combine working with children with your love of photography—and consider opening a photo studio in your home doing children's portraits. You could take a course in professional portrait techniques to get you started.

How about including an ongoing nonprofit project alongside it, as part of your give-back program? What about volunteering to work with local schoolchildren, teaching them how to take photographs of their lives as a creative and healing technique? A win-win situation, which will certainly help you get your name out there as well as create value.

70.

EXERCISE: USING MY CREATIVE FLEXIBILITY
TO ENVISION MY BUSINESS

List ways to make time again. This time let's take some of the ideas you've already got for your business and see how many different ways you can envision using them. For example:

I know I want to work with animals, and these are some of the ways I can do it:

. . . . CREATE A PROFESSIONAL DOG WALKER AGENCY...START AN ANIMAL RESCUE CENTER . . . OPEN A PET SHOP . . . LAUNCH AN INTERNET SERVICE TO FIND PEOPLE UNUSUAL PETS . . . CREATE AN ANIMAL TRAINING CENTER . . . OPEN A STABLES . . . START A NONPROFIT ORGANIZATION TO SAVE NEAR-EXTINCT EXOTIC CATS . . .

I know I want to work with . . .

71.

....

....

and these are some of the ways I can do it . . .

....

....

....

....

Once you have a list of new business possibilities, organize it in order of preference.

Now, how about looking at some different areas of business altogether? Perhaps you've always thought you wanted to start an advertising agency but now that you've spent some time opening up to your inner voice, you realize you could also be interested in running an art gallery or an agency representing talented authors or an organic restaurant.

What completely new ideas for businesses have occurred to you since you began reading this book?

I would be open to at least considering some of the following ideas as a business:

....

....

....

....

....

....

(Again after coming up with the list, organize it in order of preference.)

Now, see how your lists correspond to your SEED Vision and decide which businesses you would like to start researching in depth. Of course, once you start your research you may discover a completely new idea that appeals to you. Pay attention to what the research reveals, but don't forget to follow your instincts. Remain focused on your passions, but leave space for flexibility.

Practical Research.

We're now going to shift into left-brain mode, the more linear side of our thinking, the so-called male way of looking at a business, and begin researching the reality of what's out there in the world and how this fits in with your own vision. This could take some time if you're still working at a full-time job, but this research needs to be done as thoroughly as possible.

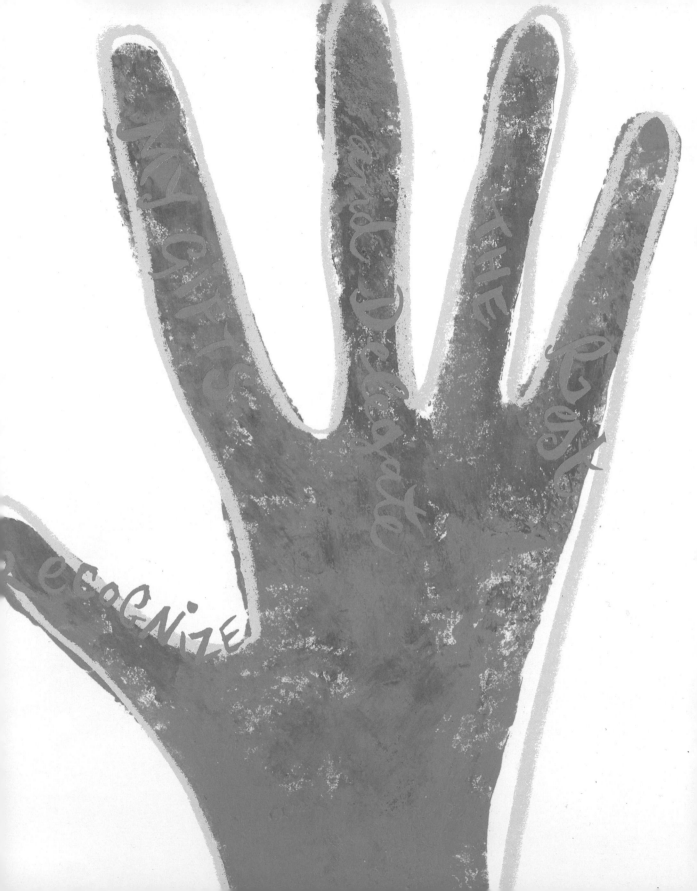

Gathering and analyzing facts and data is a very different process than the "feeling," intuitive way of going internally and working with the right brain, or feminine side, of ourselves. During this part of the vision process, you're going to use the Internet, local newspapers, trade publications and organizations, and the library to learn more about the type of business you're thinking of creating.

Here are a few initial bits of advice to start you off on your SEED enterprise research assignment:

- If you don't already do so, read the business section of your local and national newspaper on a daily basis. Keep your eye out for local and national trends, feature articles on new businesses and entrepreneurs, and anything that pertains to your potential area of business.

- Develop a relationship with a helpful librarian (at the best local library in your area) and find out where magazines and trade publications that pertain to your prospective business are kept.

- Ask a friend who's Internet-savvy to spend an evening with you surfing for the most relevant, information-rich Web sites. If you're not already an expert surfer, have your friend show you the ropes so you'll be able to navigate on your own next time. (More on the Internet later in the chapter.)

- Interview friends, friends of friends, and acquaintances—anyone who is currently engaged in the line of business you're thinking of going into. Ask them how they got started, what kind of background and experience (and funding) they had when they began, what hardships they've survived and why they love what they do.

You can certainly learn a lot from the entrepreneurial experiences of others. Consider it research as well. For example, let's say you've wanted to be a retailer for some time and while examining your passions you've realized that natural bathroom and bedroom furniture and furnishings are what you'd like to sell. Like Kathy Tissons, the founder of New York's Terre Verde eco bath and bedding store, you want to be an "ecopreneur." Talk to someone who has such a business, and then ask yourself, would you be happy standing in a store all day, being charming to the customers, training your staff, keeping track of inventory, and overseeing shipments of your product?

There are many unanticipated outside influences that can affect your enterprise—recessions, wars, property prices rising in newly fashionable areas like Soho in New York, where Kathy's beautiful shop is. But there are many unpredictable positive influences, too—it's just a case of being aware and keeping your antennas up.

The SEED Handbook gives you the opportunity, before it's too late, to change directions in your chosen enterprise. By researching the facts about your potential area of business at an early stage, you'll see for yourself which of your ideas are viable.

This is the time to find out how the type of business you want to start is doing in the marketplace. As you engage in your SEED research, focus on grounding yourself with reality, without losing your enthusiasm and confidence.

Learning How to Use the Internet.

The Internet is definitely the best place to start your research, since it has the potential to yield the greatest amount of information. Even if you don't have your own computer equipped with modem, you can gain access at your office, your local library, or even a cybercafe.

Some of you may be wondering why this section is titled "learning" to use the Internet. For many of us, myself included, the Internet is still a mystery only understood by technology-minded left-brainers and the under-eighteens.

I thought that a short explanation of how to research your potential business using new technology might be useful for all of us. I finally became fairly computer-literate over the last couple of years after running a business of fifty people, where I was the only one who had no idea how to use any of our office equipment, including computers.

I now write my articles and books on my computer and answer and send e-mail daily, but my brain starts to shut down when I anticipate the relatively simple task of searching the Net. While researching this book I decided to interview a twelve- and fourteen-year-old in my family, together with a couple of colleagues, and this is what I've found out.

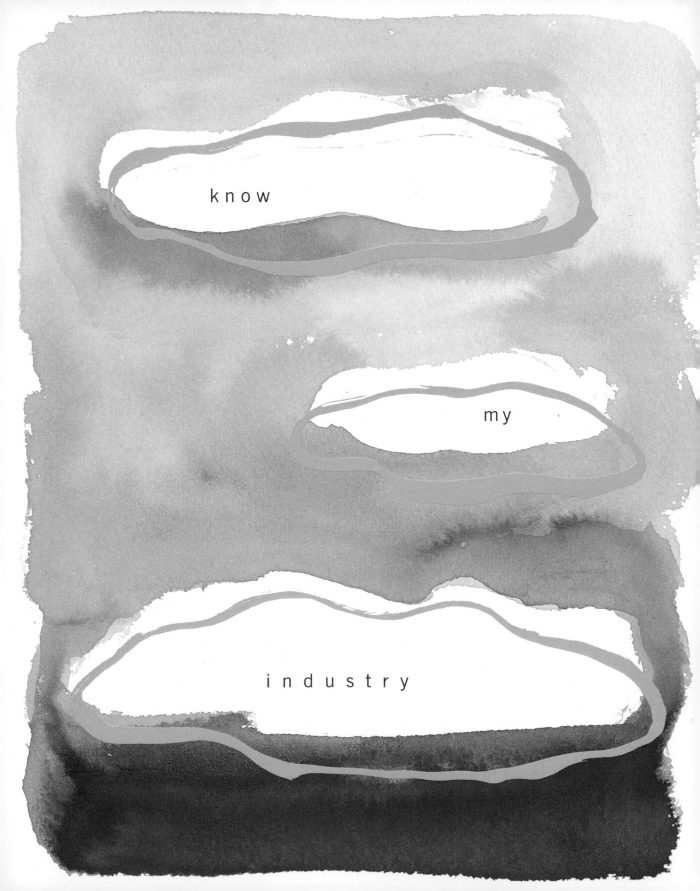

know

my

industry

To research any subject on the Internet, you have to obviously get on-line. You'll need a modem attachment that runs between your computer, an external phone or cable line, and an on-line service like Netcom., Compuserve, AOL, or Easynet. They are easy to find in any business or computer magazine, or in the phone book. You register with the one which makes the most sense, financially and geographically, pay your fees, and you'll be sent the relevant software to put on your computer. Different computers and software have varying icons and symbols—so you'll have to be shown how to "click on," a very simple process, if you don't already know how to do so.

You can avoid wasting time by researching your information through what is called a search engine, which will make it easy for you to find the specific information you're looking for. You can ask your more techno-minded friends to find the search engine that will suit you the best, depending on what information you're looking for, or check the ads in a couple of computer magazines.

The search engine will help sift through the enormous quantities of information on the Net, and the more specific you can be about what you're looking for, the more specific the information you will be given. Hoovers.com is thought to be one of the best to research businesses, for example. Yahoo.com is far more comprehensive but could probably help you with a more general search.

These search engines can refer you to loads of information. Just type in the categories you are looking for, or use the search option by typing in a word associated with your subject, and a list of topics will appear. Web sites are linked to many other sites where there is even more information available.

Most trade organizations have Web site addresses these days, as do trade publications, and every industry has Internet sites you can link into. There are also women entrepreneurs' organizations as well as quasi-official small business networks. They are easy to find on the Net—we've got some listed at the back of this book—and can be of tremendous help. There are also professional women's business groups organized according to ethnicity and these may give you information that is even more specific to you.

For example, Latina and Asian businesswomen have their own groups, and the European Organization of Black Women's Entrepreneurs has built up an extremely active lobbying group. (See back of Handbook for addresses.)

Chambers of commerce or local trade organizations are often accessible via the Internet, exist in just about every town in the world, and can be of tremendous help. And most states or governments have Internet-accessible small-business or export organizations that can help give you information in the area you are considering for your venture.

There are some very good books out on women entrepreneurs, with case histories and business advice to help you plan your new enterprise. They are mostly published in the United States but with the power of modern technology, you can order them from anywhere in the world on the Internet from amazon.com or barnesandnoble.com, if not through your local bookstores. I've read some of the best, and you'll find my recommended list at the back of the book.

Person-to-Person Research.

As you go about researching information about a business you're envisioning, don't forget that one of the best ways to gather information is to talk to people. If you're at a party or a parent-teacher meeting or even on the beach, and you happen to strike up a conversation with someone who works in the field you'd like to go into, ask her or him if theirs is a healthy industry and if it's growing. Ask them what their experience has been and what advice they have to give.

Also, find out if there are any conferences being organized for your intended industry and try to attend. Speak to as many people as you can and do some person-to-person research on the spot—or ask if you can take someone to lunch to find out more about their business.

Researching Location.

If you're considering opening up a nonvirtual business—that is, one that has an actual location—remember to do your research concerning how viable a particular spot might be for what you have in mind. Whether you're thinking of opening a hair salon, an organic food store, a florist, or a bookstore, you must appreciate that its success hinges on that old retailer's maxim, location, location, location. Foot traffic, parking, the socio-economic makeup of local residents, competing businesses in the area: All of these things must be researched.

Different aspects will influence your choice when selecting a retail property at the beginning of your search—whether it's near your home, has a cheap rent, belongs to a friend, or a similar business had already been based there. But whatever the reason, check out the practical aspects of whether it can work for you by visiting the locations constantly, at different times of the day and week to see for yourself what is happening.

For example, when my former husband opened a men's fashion shop in London in the early seventies, he selected a very cheap site at the wrong end of a fashionable street. He realized it was near the grounds of a very popular soccer club, but hadn't appreciated that most Saturday afternoons during the autumn and winter, literally millions of fans would be streaming past his shop windows, making it impossible for shoppers to get near.

80.

He also realized that there was little passing trade at that end of the street—apart from soccer fans. The plus side was that the right type of fashion-conscious, yuppy men lived near the area. He was very lucky. Through my very active public relations business, we were able to promote his original men's designer clothes in all the papers and magazines.

Customers, including many famous rock stars and actors, sought out the shop, could easily park, and would come and spend hours during the weekdays in the tiny space buying and ordering their wardrobes. He did well for a couple of years, but even so we moved our whole operation together into the then up-and-coming fashion area of Covent Garden, as soon as we could afford it.

It's unlikely that too many of you happen to have a public relations agency in the family, although we will be discussing the best ways of creating market awareness for your business later in the Handbook, with more information in the SEED books to follow. So do ask lots of questions about the background of your proposed site to other retailers in the area, real estate agencies, and anyone you can find that lives around there. This is where the local press and your chamber of commerce may be able to help, too.

Organizing Your Research.

Once you've begun to gather pertinent SEED business information, start creating files with different headings, such as "location," "sales and marketing," "financing," "design," "office equipment," and "conferences." Put clippings from trade magazines and newspapers, and any other relevant material—such as notes from your person-to-person research—in these files. Ask your friends and family to keep an eye out for articles that have to do with the business you're envisioning—you'll start accumulating valuable information that way. Also, get yourself on the list to receive newsletters that cater to people in the business you're interested in—and keep these in an accessible place.

If you're adept enough, also create a filing system on your computer. If you don't know how to do this, have a teenager in your family or some other computer-literate person help you. Keep the info and tips you've found while browsing the Net in your computer files—or you can print out the information and file it in your appropriate SEED business file.

82.

Research by Doing.

The best type of research is gained through practical experience. If you are planning to open the same kind of business that you've worked in as an employee, then you'll have less to check out. But if the business you're thinking about represents a completely new career for you, you would definitely benefit from real work experience in the field. For example, if you're considering a catering enterprise, get a job for a few months in the food service business. Learn about commercial kitchens and where and how to buy the best and cheapest supplies.

If what you'd really like to do is start up a nonprofit organization for a cause you believe in, volunteer to help out at one that appeals to you—keeping in mind that even nonprofits need an entrepreneurial approach to be successful. During your stint as a volunteer, learn as much as you can about the many complicated rules and regulations that govern this sector of the economy. At the same time, you'll be creating value by giving your time and energy to the organization from which you're learning.

MEDITATION: SEEDING THE VISION

In this part of the SEED program, we've seen how important it is to envision what we truly want to do and to gather information about the enterprise. Like a good gardener, you must find out about the variable conditions of the soil, the weather, and the light before you plant your particular variety of flower.

Now is the time to ask the Creator for clarity about how to plant the seeds of your vision so that you can obtain the most bountiful results.

Go to your special place of meditation and affirm the following thought in your own way, repeating it aloud at least once.

"I give thanks for all the valuable knowledge that is pouring into me from the universe. I affirm that I will use it clearly and wisely to create the perfect garden of my choice."

chapter 5.

Where you
consider
sustainability,
values, and
ethics as
you build
toward your
business plan.

Adding
the
Nutrients

Including your personal values and ethics in your enterprise is as important as employing your skills and incorporating your passions. Do you know which of your values are your priority and how they can work in a business context? And what does the word "sustainable" mean to you?

The answers are as important as all the other research you've been gathering, and in this chapter we'll focus on the philosophical aspect of your dream enterprise.

Let's start with "sustainable"—the S of SEED—which is, according to the Oxford Dictionary, the adjective of sustain, meaning to "support, bear the weight of, especially for a long period, encourage, nourish, endure, stand, maintain effort, corroborate." It's right next to, and connected with "sustenance," meaning nourishment, food, and means of support.

The often-quoted "sustainability," on the other hand, is not even in the dictionary. During the spiritual, political, and environmental consciousness shift of the nineties, the word "sustainable" has come to stand for something more.

It has begun to represent totally organic, environmentally sound and socially responsible commerce, and lifestyle—a tall order for us mere humans to live up to.

It's about creating new resources as you use up the old, and I can best describe it both practically and metaphorically as a garden, organic and self-sufficient, as it uses and replaces its natural supplies.

The point is that in a garden nothing natural gets wasted. The dead flowers go back to enrich the soil for the new growth, as do the dead leaves from the trees. The animals, birds, and insects that live in the garden are at one with their environment, too. They feed off the garden, help cross-pollinate the flowers, drop the seeds where they need to be planted, and even their waste matter goes back as nutrients for the land.

And the rest of nature helps as well, with embryonic plants and flowers warmed with the sun's rays and fed from the rainwater. Many organic gardeners will even plant their seeds according to the new moon, whose rhythms are said to enhance healthy growth.

Of course, hungry little critters that eat up your seedlings and bad weather can be a negative force on a garden, too—in the same way that outside influences can affect your business, despite your best intentions. We have to accept that nature, and business, has its own flow, which we can learn from to help us prepare for similar situations in the future.

Defining Sustainable Business.

Used in the SEED context, sustainability is meant to represent values-led enterprise, where environmental responsibility is taken as far as is realistically possible within your own specific business structure; human and social rights are taken into complete consideration, and there is a desire to nurture and mentor others. But none of us are perfect—I'm certainly not—and business is a particularly hard place to try and aim to be.

The sustainable "movement" is about "less being more" and "voluntary simplicity." But, let's face it, to be in business, you have to make money and, generally, to make money you have to sell your products or services within the commercial world.

E. E. Schumacher's book *Small Is Beautiful,* written in 1973, has been one of the most influential forces in the thinking of the leaders of this movement. Creating more goods for people to spend their money on is, strictly speaking, not "sustainable." The key for Schumacher was in the choice of appropriate goods and technologies that conserved materials and energy.

Can Capitalism and Sustainability Be Comfortable Bedfellows?

I've spent a lot of time, over the past seven years or so, questioning the reality of how to create a sustainable enterprise, both for myself in the communications and public relations sector, as well as in the context of this book.

I have been fortunate enough to either hear or read about sustainability, together with the new twenty-first-century way of transformational business, from some of the world's greatest experts on the subject. I have listed some of the best books to read on the subject at the back of the Handbook and have also asked some of these experts for general pointers for the SEED entrepreneurs as you begin to plan your sustainable enterprise.

Hazel Henderson, one of the world's foremost futurists and economists, has long been one of my mentors, and wrote the foreword to *The SEED Handbook*. She says she considers a sustainable business one that strives to produce goods and services that meet real needs at a personal and spiritual level, while conserving natural resources and even restoring the environment.

These include businesses committed to personal development, less toxic foods and lifestyles, more satisfying relationships, healthier environments, closer-knit communities, and higher overall quality of life.

Jonathon Porritt is considered one of the U.K.'s foremost spokespeople on sustainability and the environment, advising government, the corporate world, and educational establishments on sustainability through the organization he cofounded, Forum for the Future.

Jonathon is a master at networking and bringing together people from the public sector of local and national government, big business, and individual activists. He told me, "One should never really start a business without real love and respect for the business organism one is about to bring into the world."

Anita Roddick is well known all over the world as the founder of The Body Shop, the international chain of beauty product shops, whose policies toward human rights and the environment have always been at the top of their business agenda.

Anita told me of sustainable practices in business meant many things to her. "It means auditing your environmental practices. It means cleaning up your own mess. It means doing everything possible to lessen the environmental impact. And this is done by way of

a process of auditing, measuring, being accountable, and being transparent. Supporting the local economic community, especially farmers, anywhere and everywhere in the world. Finally it means turning the workplace into not only a place for the production of goods, but also a place that encourages the productivity of the human spirit."

Gunter Pauli, founder of Belgium-based, environmentally friendly household cleaning products, Ecover, e-mailed me his perspective on sustainable entrepreneurship when he returned home briefly during his nonstop crusade of starting small community enterprises founded on sustainable principles in Third World countries across the planet.

"Anything, anyone alive, creates waste. That is not the problem. Doing nothing with it is the problem. You cannot expect the earth to produce more; you must do more with what the earth produces."

He added, "After decades of reusing products, reducing waste, recycling left-overs, we know that it is not enough. We have to emulate nature, where whatever is waste for one, is food for another. Nothing gets wasted."

90.

Hunter and Amory Lovins, the respected wife and husband authorities on sustainability, who have long been exploring the subject at their Rocky Mountain Institute, a forty person resources policy center in Colorado, sent me some pointers for SEED.

They have just written a new book with Paul Hawken, best-selling author of *The Ecology of Commerce*, called *Natural Capitalism* due out in April 2000 from publisher Little Brown, which, even before publication, is causing ripples across the sustainable business industry.

They told me that the basic principles of *Natural Capitalism* are:

- radically increased resource efficiency

- eliminating the concept of waste by redesigning the economy on biological lines that close the loops of material flow

- shifting the structure of the economy from focusing on the processing of materials and the making of things to the creation of service and flow

- reversing the planetary destruction now underway with programs of restoration that invest in natural capital

Paul Hawken altered the thinking of many visionary business leaders in his book *The Ecology of Commerce*, which he first published in 1993, with HarperCollins. In it he argued that "corporations, because they are the dominant institution on the planet, must squarely face the social and environmental problems that afflict humankind."

Paul listed eight commitments for a corporation to take on board to be considered sustainable:

1. To reduce absolute consumption of energy and natural resources among developed countries by eighty percent within forty to sixty years.

2. To provide secure, stable, and meaningful employment for people everywhere.

3. To be self-actuating, as opposed to regulated, controlled, mandated, or moralistic.

4. To honor human nature and market principles.

5. To perceive a sustainable world as more desirable than our present way of life.

6. To exceed sustainability by restoring degraded habitats and ecosystems to their fullest biological capacity.

7. To rely on current solar income.

8. To be fun and engaging, and strive for an aesthetic outcome.

91.

These theories may seem far away from the small enterprise that you want to start. But I've always found that since I've been aware of the larger, global picture of a positive future, I'm clearer about the way I can, in my small way, adapt my own business to sustainable principles.

Putting sustainable principles into practical applications is not always easy for start-up entrepreneurs. However, if you can integrate such principles as you plan your business, you will find it far easier as you grow.

TEN Seed TIPS ON HOW TO BECOME A SUSTAINABLE BUSINESS

On a day-to-day basis, there may be many simple ways you can incorporate a sense of environmental and social responsibility into your business.

I've put a list together of just a few practical, sustainable ideas that you can apply during the early stages of setting up your SEED enterprise, and I'm sure that you have many other ideas as well.

1. Use recycled or wood-free (such as hemp) paper for your stationery or commit to finance the replanting of an equivalent number of trees to the paper you use annually, as we have in this book

2. Ensure that neither you or any of your suppliers use exploitative labor.

3. Be conservative in your use of energy—both in your offices and in your use of transport.

4. Check that your bank is not investing in corrupt Third World governments or industries that are environmentally harmful.

5. Contribute your time and a portion of your profit, where appropriate, to nonprofit causes.

6. Think of your business as a biological organism, where even the waste can be used in some way. Recycle!

7. Create communication and value in some way in your community.

8. Avoid the use of unnecessary toxic chemicals in your business, whether in the finished product or in your office.

9. Treat your staff with respect, and profit-share where possible.

10. Create a business environment that is healthy and attractive, and that will benefit the well being of those that work in or visit it.

There are some wonderful ideas in the inspiring, and constantly updated, book *The New Natural House Book* by David Pearson about how to create a healthy workplace. Published by Simon & Schuster in the U.S., and Conran Octopus Books in the U.K., the book contains some excellent tips on being ecologically sound in the office.

Among them is advice on using low-voltage halogen uplights, or full spectrum or compact fluorescent desk lamps, if you have to use anything other than the preferred natural light. Pearson also suggests avoiding plastic products and accessories, synthetic furnishings and carpets, toxic cleaning aids, glues, fixatives, and aerosols.

EXERCISE: HOW MY BUSINESS COULD BE SUSTAINABLE

We've listed just a few tips that you could incorporate into your business planning, but you can probably think of quite a few more yourself. During your next quiet times in front of your SEED altar, ask your higher self or intuition for ways you can infuse your own ideas on sustainability within your business.

My ideas to incorporate sustainability into my business are:

94.

....

....

....

....

....

....

....

....

....

As your enterprise grows, there will be many opportunities presented for you to incorporate different aspects of sustainability.

Irresponsible Business Practices = Bad Karma, but Good Practices Are Good for Business.

Conversely, there are ways that you can, unknowingly, make business decisions that can have a negative effect on the environment or society. It's a trap that many big corporations constantly get caught in.

The substantial amount of negative publicity that has been generated in the last few years concerning some of the world's largest corporations and their "so-called" irresponsible business practices has resulted in many questions being raised inside the business community.

Situations concerning exploitive child and women labor, cooperation with corrupt governments, environmental damage caused by corporate greed, and other harmful practices have caused many companies to self-examine and answer to internal or external audits of the way they do business.

Major corporations, which always thought they were "nice guys," have seen how ignorance of some of their branches' or suppliers' business practices can have a devastating effect on both their share price as well as their relationship with their customers.

For example, Nike has instigated very high ethical standards regarding their environmental and manufacturing policies after a campaign by the media regarding "sweatshop" production of their shoes by some of their factories.

Likewise, Shell suffered a lot of bad press after the executions in Nigeria of writer Ken Saro-Wiwa and seven other members of the Ogoni tribe. Shell was seen as hand-in-hand with the corrupt Nigerian government by the outside world. Shell executives were genuinely shocked at the reaction, as they did not consider themselves responsible, but they reacted quickly.

They set themselves a new code of conduct, based on the highest of principles regarding human rights, and admit that it was only because of a public relations disaster that they examined this side of their business. Now, they are constantly striving, as one of the world's largest corporations, to keep their values and ethics at the front end of their business.

95.

The good news is that many large international companies now consider "good" business practices to be good for business, good for society, and good for the environment.

Values, Ethics, and Honesty in Your SEED Business.

What the large companies have been forced to realize by default—that you need to run your business along the principles that you'd like to apply to all aspects of your life—is an easy principle for you to implant in your business plan while you're still designing your SEED enterprise.

It's essentially a matter of creating positive value, and to do so you need to make sure the sustainable nutrients of values, ethics, and honesty are in place before you lock in too many of your business practices. Otherwise your SEED venture may have an unintended toxic effect on some part of society or our environment.

Not everybody wants to be an ecopreneur and start an organic restaurant or make natural fiber clothing or housewear. (Although I must point out that the environmental industry and eco-products are expanding rapidly into one of the most exciting and profitable areas of twenty-first-century business!)

You may want to run a corner manicurist shop, as many thousands of Asian immigrants are successfully doing in the United States. Still, it'll be your decision whether or not to use less toxic products and to pay your employees well. Or you may want to start an office sandwich-delivery service where most of your customers prefer white bread, but you can still make it the healthiest and tastiest version of white bread than you can!

The S in SEED for sustainable is whatever works for you and should be in accordance with your own personal values and ethics.

What Do You Value? What Are Your Ethics?

In trying to analyze the difference between values and ethics, I spoke to a number of people whom, I believe, honor both in all areas of their lives: personal, professional, and community.

They all agreed that values are a guideline to how you want to live your life, your standards, and your internal belief system. Your ethics, or set of moral principles, are what you apply outside yourself; they are about how you interact with others.

For far too long, the traditional business world has encouraged a very different set of values for the office than the ones you would apply in your personal life. Such a system, by its very nature, creates intense stress from having to live a "split personality" life.

In the traditional old paradigm business world, profit and share price were all that mattered. People were merely statistics, and executives of major companies made decisions, often harshly, that sometimes had devastating effects on people's lives or the environment.

98.

Such callous, corporate attitudes are partly why so many people, particularly women, are today leaving the corporate world to start their own businesses, where their personal values can be an inclusive part of their professional life.

We lose a crucial part of ourselves when we don't "practice what we preach" or act on what we deeply believe.

How much less stressful and more enjoyable to work in a way that is sympathetic with your inner belief system. It not only gives you a feeling of wholeness; it affects your enterprise in a positive way, too.

For example, if one of your values is to be generous, then why not be open, even when speaking to your competitors? I used to be far more competitive when I was younger, but now I enjoy speaking to colleagues who work in similar fields. I am happy to give them information or contacts that they can use, knowing that people are always doing the same for me.

If what you value the most is being honest, then for goodness sake, put this at the center of your business plan. I believe that companies based on truth and integrity will always come to the top rather than those based on half-truths and manipulation.

So often businesses are scared of telling the truth, particularly when they have something serious to hide and are not prepared for change. Again, this is a short-term attitude that will do more harm than good in the end.

At the same time, I am not suggesting you go around telling anyone who will listen to you the most intimate details of your enterprise and finances. I personally have never cared about keeping secrets, but that sort of honesty policy is a matter of individual choice! We all have different sets of values, and what is important to us shifts as we get older and our circumstances change.

You may value creativity . . . and your way of incorporating this value into your business may be to enable your employees to be as creative as they can by giving them flexibility in the way they do their jobs. Or perhaps your highest value is time spent with your children . . . so you can make sure that you allow those with whom you work to have the time to spend with theirs.

99.

So what are your personal values? And how would you prioritize them? Which values influence almost every decision you make in your life? Which keep your inner being in balance? And how do these values relate to your business ethics, to the way you intend to interact with people and the marketplace?

Using some of the examples below to inspire you, list your values and then go back and number the list according to which values are most important to you.

EXAMPLE

The values I want to live and work by are:

- The Three R's: respect for self, respect for others, and responsibility for my actions

- Always paying my bills on time

- Bringing beauty into the world

- Balancing work and personal time

- Healing others

- Using my leadership qualities

- Creating a pleasant environment

Next, start making a list of the words and phrases that you've either read or thought about that best express your feelings on sustainability, values, and ethics. Save the list and keep it in a "SEED Values" file, to refer to later. Once you've had time to assimilate these values and feel which of them are your priorities, they are going to be used in your mission statement, the first part of your business plan.

Now is the time to go to your special SEED garden, or altar, for quiet time, where your thoughts will settle back into your unconscious, to be grounded and nurtured in a sustainable environment.

102.

MEDITATION TO GROUND YOUR VALUES AND NURTURE YOUR ETHICS

During your silent moments today and in the coming weeks, feel the sense of wholeness that is to come from your business and your personal life.

Ask the universe to integrate your life fully so that your personal values and business vision can be totally at one, and your most basic belief system and professional ambitions can work in harmony.

In your own words, or using this SEED affirmation, repeat out loud a prayer for harmonious balance between your work and your values.

"I ask for the strength to integrate all aspects of my life so that my values and professional ambitions go hand in hand."

chapter

6.

Where we assess the most crucial business tools of all—your intuition and physical well being—as well as the necessary practical equipment and tools of your trade.

Organising

your tool shed

In this chapter we are going to look at the basic office tools you will need if you are planning a service-oriented enterprise as well as look at how to go about researching the most suitable equipment for a more complex business.

Either way, this is the time in the SEED program where you start thinking of the practical tools that you are going to need to get your enterprise started.

But before you do that, we are going to take a look at the two other crucial tools that you will be using to create your SEED enterprise and beyond—your intuition and physical well being.

106. Your Intuition As a Business Tool.

Throughout the Handbook, we've been working with your intuition to ensure that what your mind is telling you is in balance with the vision from your "soul" or inner being.

Now, in a more conscious way, we will look at refining your intuition skills so that you trust the signposts that your intuitive self is pointing out to you.

The longer I stay an entrepreneur, the more lessons I get about trusting the natural flow my life seems to be taking and not trying to control situations only from my head. Of course, that doesn't mean I let negative situations continue when they arise, but I have learned to trust the bigger picture of my life and view the situation as a whole. Even at my darkest moments, I remind myself that I am going through a process of learning and to listen to my inner voice.

On a personal or professional basis, we all have our dark times, when we feel blocked for all sorts of reasons. It's only by letting go and releasing control that the space is created to allow in positive change. We have to learn to TRUST our flow and listen to our intuition.

Intuition and Giant Cabbages: The Findhorn Garden.

A wonderful metaphor, which explains how depression or creative blocks can be valuable, was told to me a few years ago by Eileen Caddy, cofounder of the Findhorn Foundation. Now in her late seventies, Eileen and her former husband, Peter, created the foundation in Scotland in the sixties, where it became one of the foremost spiritual ecocommunities in the world.

Eileen told me that she can get very deep depressions and realized some years ago that when she did, it was as if new seeds were germinating which needed the dark to strengthen.

Her darkest moments always preceded some enormous breakthrough for her, which she saw as beautiful flowers blooming in the sunshine.

Findhorn has a well-known history with gardens and listening, or tuning into, your inner voice. When Eileen, Peter, and a third colleague, Dorothy Maclean, first founded the community in the bleakness of a sandy caravan park on the north-east coast of Scotland near Inverness, they made many business decisions about how to run the community based on information that Eileen intuited through her inner voice. The problem that Eileen had in the early years was finding somewhere quiet to go that allowed her the space to get into a meditative state.

Eileen, Peter, and Dorothy, together with her three boisterous young sons, were all living together in a small mobile home. She ended up most nights in the campground's public lavatory, where she spent the small hours of the morning listening to her inner voice or as she viewed it, "God." One message she "heard" for the community said that "one garden can save a world." An inspiring thought for your SEED enterprise.

Dorothy Maclean started a garden on the inhospitable soil, where she grew the growing community's "famous" gigantic cabbages and other larger-than-life vegetables. Dorothy used to communicate with the devas, or spirits of the plants and vegetables, asking them intuitively how they wanted to be cared for and watered. Whether you believe that plants and all living things have their own spirits or not, the Findhorn Garden became world-renowned for its incredible produce. Hundreds of thousands of visitors still continue to visit the center to see the results for themselves and participate in the experience of living in a spiritual community.

I went there myself several years ago and had some practical experience on how each work party starts their sessions with a lit candle, some quiet tuning-in time, followed by a brief sharing of what's going on for each individual.

I use the same process to start our workday at Globalfusion, my new start-up enterprise, where I'm working with a new, young team on global P.R. and communication. We find it a very dynamic way to bring the team together as well as an opportunity for us all to connect with our own inner voices.

Of course, the feminine way of doing things has always largely been based on intuition. It is only just now that the left-brain business world is starting to appreciate how effective the instinctive way of doing business can be, provided it is grounded in reality.

EXERCISE: KEEPING YOUR INTUITIVE IDEAS
IN A SEED JOURNAL

Even if you already keep a journal, it's time to start one that specifically pertains to your SEED enterprise. In this journal you'll be jotting down your instinctive ideas, dreams, drawings, and thoughts to be drawn on later as your garden begins to take shape.

Journal writing not only helps you keep track of intuitive ideas, but as Julie Cameron so brilliantly describes in the "morning pages" section of her book *The Artist's Way*, it's also a way to overcome any creative blocks. When you get into the pleasant habit of writing in your journal every day, you'll find that your unconscious mind will supply you with innovative thoughts and guideposts that will help you formulate the next stages of your SEED project.

Earlier in *The SEED Handbook*, we talked about the importance of gathering relevant information from the commercial world, which now should be in the appropriate virtual or physical file. You've also been digging hard through the soil of your own unconscious, and by now your SEED Vision poster or scrapbook should be giving you a very definite picture of your SEED enterprise.

Thinking through the specifics of your business is going to require an even more focused

approach, as you decipher the answers to your entrepreneurial questions. You'll be delighted to discover that these answers will often appear in some unexpected places, including your journal and even your dreams. For example, you might be wondering where the best location is for your children's art school—should you hold the classes in your home or try to find an inexpensive yet appropriate space? After weighing each possibility with regard to cost and practical considerations, your early morning journal entry "delivers" the answer to you in the form of a riddle, a poem, or a sketch.

The point is, as you start making significant decisions, your practical research needs to be backed up by your own gut feeling—and those intuitive feelings can be accessed by such activities as journal writing.

I would recommend you keep your SEED journal by your bed at night, so you can record any dreams or early morning thoughts that may answer specific questions you asked your unconscious mind before going to sleep.

110.

Nothing is set in stone—as a wise woman said to me once, "My final decision is never
my last," and you can always change direction. But now is the time to fully open up to
your intuition, and be sure that your instincts agree with your intellectual process about
whether your enterprise is the right one for you.

Write down your concept in a few words in your SEED journal and focus on the words
during your quiet time every day, as well as before you go to sleep. Ask the powers of
your unconscious to let you know, either through your dreams or the drifting thoughts of
a relaxed mind, if you are on the right track or if there are changes to make. Make note
of the words and images that come through to you from your meditation or dreams by
putting them into your journal.

Over a period of a month or so, continue to visualize yourself at work within your dream
enterprise. Get used to asking your "inner voice" to give you the answers to any of your
questions regarding personal and business decisions that you have to make, and become
accustomed to going inward for the answers.

We Can All Be Zeitgeists: A Final Word on Intuition.

I have always used my intuition to "sense" my way into new ideas. The word zeitgeist,
used particularly in the fashion world, where I worked for many years, and even applied
to me by the British press on occasion, refers to a person who reflects "the spirit of the
times." Someone who seems to pull new ideas, designs, colors, and trends seemingly out

111.

of thin air, often simultaneously with other forecasters.

I've seen this happen too often in the fashion and design worlds, to believe that it's not just coincidence—which I never believe in, anyway. When we're sensitive and open-minded to it, we can all tap into this collective stream—and we can then use this "information" to help us plan our own unique enterprise.

Your Body as Your Essential Tool.

Your health and well being is always important, but opening your own business could put your body under tremendous extra pressures and stress, if you're not careful.

During the first years of setting up your own enterprise, you are going to be pushing your body to the limits. Let's face it. Opening your own business means you are going to be working hard, long hours, often over a hot computer, with potentially stressful situations frequently hovering around.

Now is the time to introduce some simple stress-management exercises and habits into your life, which will help you thrive even during the most arduous period.

We've already talked about clearing out bad eating habits in Chapter One, and it's even more important at this stage. Eating regular meals, as little junk food as possible, taking some good supplements, and drinking six to eight glasses of pure water a day will help to ensure this good health and strength you'll need to get your new enterprise underway.

We all have our weaknesses though. I love almost all food, although my particular vice is chocolate. I've had it explained to me that when you use a lot of adrenaline—and I, like many entrepreneurs, do—the sugar moves out of your blood cells, encouraging a sweet tooth or in my case, a chocolate craving.

There are, however, healthier ways of satisfying your sugar cravings. Raw carrots are the way one of my colleagues alleviates her sugar needs, and healthy fiber bars also fill that gap.

When I'm busy at meetings and working in teams, I'm not aware of hunger at all. It's thinking and writing time that does it to me. (This chapter has seen several packets of

natural carrot corn chips disappearing into my mouth.)

However, I've also gone for an hour's hike today, mostly uphill, and danced around my room to one of my favorite dance albums by the British group Faithless. Of course, one of the advantages of working from home is that you can go hiking in the middle of the day or just turn on some loud music and dance when the pressure gets too much.

I cannot overemphasize to any SEED entrepreneur the importance of exercise and body maintenance. Don't ever underestimate how much long-term time you can save by staying healthy.

Whether it's an early gym session, regular massage, or yoga lesson, it's absolutely crucial to stay conscious of your body's need to stretch, move, and relax.

I have always been addicted to dancing from my early teens, and when possible I practice the Five Rhythms' program of teacher and author Gabrielle Roth. Starting with a feminine flow, moving to a more assertive masculine style, on to the intense third "chaotic" rhythm, then to childlike lyrical, and finishing in the still of meditation, Gabrielle's work builds up to some lively action and then brings you back to a sacred space.

I've seen children, disabled men and women in wheelchairs, seniors, and men and women of all ages become agile and inspired by Gabrielle's work, and I would recommend her program to everyone. Going through the "Five Rhythms" completely refreshes me—and lets me know that my mind, body, and soul are one.

We do need to get out of our minds and consciously into our bodies regularly, to be the most effective in our jobs. I believe in regular holidays, quiet time, lunch breaks, loo breaks (instead of taking that next "urgent" phone call), simple activities such as cycling, swimming, yoga, tennis, and at least twenty minutes of walking a day, preferably in nature, or at the very least, walking up the stairs to your meetings instead of taking the elevator.

I'm not suggesting you try all the above—you'd never have the time. I certainly don't. But I do think it's important to engage in one physical activity a day, as well as your quiet time, to maintain balance in your life.

Aside from getting adequate daily exercises and spending some quiet time alone every day, what should you avoid in order to prevent physical imbalance or illness? I speak from experience when I recommend that SEED entrepreneurs stay away from:

LATE NIGHTS

EXCESSIVE EATING

EXCESSIVE DRINKING OF ALCOHOL

TOO MUCH COFFEE

NEGATIVE PEOPLE

If you have trouble sticking to a healthy regimen, just remind yourself how important your well being is to your new enterprise. If you're not healthy, it won't be either.

Some Physical Tips to Keep You Stretched and Healthy.

I invited Celina Marquez, the delightful young woman who has taken on the responsibility of teaching me yoga and stretch exercises when I am in L.A., to work out some simple exercises which any of us can do.

The first four she describes should be done every hour or so as you sit in front of your computer.

SEED Exercises to Do in Front of a Computer:

- Brain Refresher—Sit in your chair and drop your upper body toward the floor. The blood will rush to the brain bringing essential oxygen to clear away the cobwebs. Hold the pose for a few seconds. Repeat three times.

- Head Clasp—Interlace your hands at base of neck and pull head down gently. This will immediately help a stiff neck. Hold for about ten seconds. Repeat three times.

- Head Rolls—Roll your head slowly to the left, in a circular motion. Repeat the same process to the right. Repeat three times. You may hear some soft clicks, which means your neck is loosening up.

- Shoulder Shrugs—Raise your shoulders to your ears, hold for three seconds, and release. Repeat three times. Your shoulders should feel completely relaxed after this brief exercise.

These simple exercises can work for you wherever you are. I find them useful for long plane journeys or any situation which tends to result in a stiff neck and shoulders.

Keep improving my technology Skills

SEED Stretching Exercises.

Celina has also designed three special SEED full-body exercises for you to do first thing in the morning and any other time of the day, when you feel that your whole body needs a simple stretch.

118.

- Waist Bend—Stand with feet apart at shoulder width. Keeping arms as straight as possible, raise arms above head and press palms together. Bend from the waist slowly to one side, then the other. Breathe normally. Repeat three times.

- Reach and Drop—Stand with feet shoulder width apart and raise arms straight up above shoulders. Keeping heels on the ground and looking past your hands, reach up as far as possible. Reach for five counts then let body drop forward with knees bent and head relaxed. Hold for five counts. Repeat three times.

- Sitting Waist Twist and Leg Stretch—Sit on the floor with legs spread as wide apart as comfortable. Bend forward from the waist and feel the stretch through the back of the legs. Place your right hand on left leg and try to touch your chest to your left knee. Repeat other side. Repeat twice.

The Tools of Your Trade.

Your practical tools will obviously vary according to the industry and enterprise you've decided on. However, most businesses need certain basic office essentials, such as a computer, fax, and telephone.

By now, I hope you will have realized how important it is to have a computer, whatever your business. Even though it was possible to do your earlier research on the Internet from libraries, or cybercafes, the time has come for you to invest in a computer, new or recycled. They are becoming more and more essential for daily life, as well as necessary for doing your general correspondence, including the increasingly popular e-mail. Once you're up and running, your computer should also contain your database of contacts and all your financial information.

There always seems to be much dialogue about whether to buy a Mac or an IBM compatible computer, known as a PC. I've got both and don't see what the big difference is. Basically, if you're going to do more creative work, that requires presentation skills, buy a Mac. They are more flexible for this kind of work. If your work's going to be more linear, containing lots of financial details, choose the more appropriate PC.

A basic laptop will cost you from one thousand dollars or about fifteen hundred pounds upwards in the U.K. Computers are cheaper in the U.S. than the U.K., so if you're not based there and you're planning a holiday in the States, consider buying one there. You just have to watch the different spell-checks. You'll need some good software, too, for basic office needs, like Microsoft Office, which is now available for all types of computers.

Remember, too, that it's getting easier all the time to lease a computer, together with much of your other office equipment. That way you can have your model updated, free of charge, and you can pay the costs off over a period of time rather than in one lump sum.

If you're going for recycled computers, look again on the Internet, or the local classified press for a good bargain. Don't buy anything without a good friend who knows about computers checking it out.

If necessary, borrow your husband's or your children's computer, but make that only a short-term loan unless they rarely use it. Just imagine the chaos, if you all want to get on at the same time or somebody else accidentally wipes out some crucial notes.

120.

Even if your office is in your home, you'll also need:

- a printer for the computer

- fax machine

- desk

- a comfortable chair

- filing cabinet

- bulletin board

And—if you live in a busy household—a second phone line.

You'll need stationery even at this early phase of your SEED enterprise, but until you finalize the name of your company and where you'll ultimately be located, this will merely be your interim stationery. Just use your personal name, and include your home address or a postal address, along with your phone number, fax number, and e-mail address on some official-looking letterhead. You can either print this on your computer or have it printed at any local photocopier or print shop.

Business cards are an essential networking and researching tool. Again, just have your personal details on the card and make it readable and clean looking. There is software available to do this on your computer, or they can be printed inexpensively at local printers.

You also need the smaller office utensils for your desk, the stapler: the paperclips, and of course the little yellow Post-its, so no one, including you, forgets your messages. And then there are, of course, the specific tools for your chosen business. It is important to re-emphasize here how easy it is to buy recycled professional equipment at reasonable prices through the Internet and the classified trade and consumer press.

This is another instance where practical experience or educational training in your chosen field will be beneficial. Not only will you know what equipment works best, you'll know the best—and most reasonable—places to buy it.

Start making a list of all the items and tools you are going to need to open your business. Include a shopping list for your basic office equipment and keep the list in a virtual or actual file titled "My Tools." Then start tearing ads or information about new or secondhand equipment from specialist magazines, Internet sites, and the local press as well as collecting stationery catalogues to put in your file.

At this point, you're getting a feel for the best "value for money" prices for the tools and equipment you'll need to enable you to start preparing a budget.

122.

MEDITATION: TO AFFIRM THE TOOLS OF THE UNIVERSE

Return to your sacred SEED quiet place to ground the many ideas and thoughts that this chapter has provoked.

Start using all your tools consciously in your daily life. Remember to use your SEED journal to record your intuitive thoughts as you move forward on the path toward opening your own business. Keep your body supple and healthy, and expand your technical skills in your chosen area. Acknowledge the wholeness of your mind, body, and spirit and repeat this SEED Affirmation aloud, or create your own.

"I give thanks to the universe and acknowledge the wholeness of all aspects of my life, enabling me to find the sustainable tools I need to create my enterprise."

I will radiate to all

areas of my life

and Honor my true

worth. I am ready

to receive the bouquets

that I deserve.

chapter 7

Seed Money

Where we look at the practical aspects of budgets, barter, and banks, together with what money means to you personally

Does the subject of money bring up your fears about self-worth? Do you see money purely as a form of energy to create your dreams? Or is earning a fortune your prime motivation for starting a business?

So many of us become uncomfortable, even creatively blocked, when talking about money. Financial independence is one of the main reasons given by many entrepreneurs for starting a business. Being in control of how you earn your living and how you manage your own finances is one of the most empowering experiences that one can have, and any human being is capable of it in today's world.

Yet there are still many countries where social and cultural conditions don't allow many people—women in particular—this freedom. Where, in fact, women are considered the possessions of their husbands or fathers.

126.

Even within these societies, however, we hear inspiring stories of women entrepreneurs who, using the facilities of micro-lending from community banks and nongovernmental organizations (NGOs), together with the support of grass-roots networks, start small businesses that can finance their children's education and put roofs over their families heads.

There has been much research done on the results of micro-finance, now used in many Third-World countries as a more effective alternative to straightforward aid, and in both Eastern and Western societies, the borrowers, mainly women, have a pay-back rate of well over 90 percent.

These women don't have the choice whether or not to start their own businesses. They have to make money work for them if they and their families are to survive. Those of us who are born into more fortunate circumstances really have little excuse. Regardless of the sexist or stereotypical conditioning you may have been brought up with, now is the moment to seize your power and bring your finances under your own control.

It's important to remember that financing a business doesn't have to be a mystery. The basic rules are: Whatever money's coming in has to cover whatever money is going out, and you've got to have access to enough money to initially fund your enterprise without becoming financially strapped.

Plus a healthy enterprise can grow without just using conventional money. We're going to look at other highly successful ways to make the economics of your business work, such as the increasingly popular community systems of barter, LET, and local money, where goods and services are exchanged in kind.

The Value of Money.

Before we delve into the practical aspects of finance, let's take a look at your personal attitudes toward money. Have you always been considered very extravagant or do you find it easy to stretch your money a long way? Do you have a history of literally losing cash or checks? Do you enjoy gambling?

Do you find it difficult in your current situation to ask for more money, either from your boss or from your partner? Do you like giving gifts but not receiving them? Do you think it's possible that on some level you don't think you deserve abundance in your life?

I'd like to use myself as an example for a moment, and share with you how some of my attitudes about money have reverberated in my business life. After my marriage of many years to my business partner broke up, I learned a number of financial lessons by trial and error. I'd relied on my ex-husband to arrange all our financial affairs—something too many of us women find easy to do. Once I was on my own, I had to start being responsible for my own finances again, and I made some stupid mistakes.

I trusted other people when I should have been more cautious. They convinced me to either invest against my better judgement or give them power to sign checks on my behalf.

I let other people read the small print in documents for me or I just didn't bother. I was sloppy and lazy about financial details and in the same way that I didn't bother to learn how to use a computer, I let other people handle financial matters for me.

I deserved what I got. But I've wised up. Having started again in a new country with two small start-up businesses, and going through the process of putting a new, trustworthy team of advisers around me, I realized that this time around I intend to value myself, my work, and my money. I always read the small print in my contracts, keep a close eye on the money that comes and goes in my businesses, and don't make unwise investments.

Having said that, I'm still not the greatest when it comes to negotiating money. I say "yes" too easily and then regret it afterward. Looking at this aspect of my personality, I see this trait as a part of my "people-pleaser" pattern. Now I'm training myself to think things over before recklessly agreeing.

That's not to say that I now believe in being mean or greedy in business, either with my time or money. I do believe that the people working for or with me should be fairly paid as much as the situation can stand. I just don't intend to be irresponsible about money anymore.

The reason that I'm sharing my money hang ups with you is that I'm sure that I'm not alone in my patterns. How many of you have made mistakes over money because you wanted to please others or because of laziness, fear, or trusting the wrong people?

128.

EXERCISE: HOW TO RECOGNIZE YOUR MONEY PATTERNS

Think of a time when you've had to ask for money that you deserve. Perhaps when you wanted a raise at work or when you were owed money or when a prospective employer or client asked you how much you'd like to be paid.

Did you find it easy to come up with what you considered a fair amount or did you find it difficult even asking? Are you aware that you may have a problem receiving what you are entitled to?

Write down in your journal some particularly memorable or even painful experiences you've had when asking for money. Does a pattern emerge? Is the very common problem of self-worth present in your life? Because if it is, it's time for a major shift. Recognizing your value is an essential part of being a SEED entrepreneur.

Marleen McDaniel, the CEO and chair of the highly successful Internet destination Women.com, based just outside San Francisco, who I met while researching the Handbook, has launched five start-up companies.

She told me that she has had to raise much of the finances for her companies herself. She said that for every dollar that she's raised, she's been turned down five. "I've had to find millions over the years and if I get turned down, I just move on to the next situation. You have to remember in business that it's nothing personal."

Marleen has never doubted her worth, or her companies', and has earned a considerable amount of money for herself and her businesses over the years. She believes her confidence comes from her parents, both positive people, who convinced her she could do anything she wanted from an early age.

So many of our patterns regarding self-worth and money do come from our relationship with our parents and their own attitude toward money. For example there was an attitude prevalent forty or fifty years ago amongst the parents of the baby boomers that "you get what you're given" and should be "satisfied with your lot." Such thinking would obviously discourage you from breaking the mold and striving to create something new.

Also, some of us may have grown up in families where parents didn't want their children to surpass them financially, or didn't teach daughters to be confident about making money. Regardless of your particular cultural or family background, it's time now to recognize who you are and value yourself for it.

It is time to affirm your self-worth on a daily basis. There are many ways of doing this, but the most powerful is to repeat this simple affirmation to yourself several times during your quiet time.

SEED AFFIRMATION OF SELF-VALUE

"I add value to all areas of my life and honor my true worth. I am ready to receive all the bouquets that I deserve."

Many of you, of course, may be more like Marleen McDaniel and not have this kind of self-worth blockage. You may be fully confident about your value to the universe, both in financial terms and in terms of service toward your fellow beings. In fact, money may not be very important to you other than as a useful way to turn the wheels.

But whatever your personal attitudes toward money, it is essential to be aware of them before you start your SEED business. If you need to strengthen your feelings of self-worth or shift away from discouraging messages you may have received during your childhood, spend some extra time with the previous affirmation. If you already have a healthy perspective about your ability to earn and manage your own money, appreciate that about yourself and recognize how it's going to help you as you plant your new business.

Creating a Budget

130.

No matter what kind of business you're starting—even a non profit one—if it's not funded properly, it won't be around very long. All economic aspects of your SEED enterprise must be well thought out and organized, with as much planning into the future as possible.

Here are the basics:

- You need to calculate the amount of money you require to start up your business and where that money might come from: your own savings, personal loans from friends or family, investors, the bank, or—as many small entrepreneurs have done—your credit cards.

- You've got to estimate what your costs are going to be every month, and when and how you expect to bring the money in to cover them.

- You must consider how you're going to finance your overheads and personal life while you're in the process of getting your business to a profitable stage.

Let's start with your personal living costs. Calculate how much you will need to keep yourself for the first six months of your start-up. Cover your basic costs—rent and utilities (or the percentage of your home overheads that you're not using for work), food, entertainment, medical and dental, transportation, holidays, clothes, and any other areas of personal expenditure.

EXERCISE: BUDGETING MY PERSONAL EXPENSES

List all your personal expenses, using some of the suggestions below as a guideline. Next, write the approximate amounts you spend on each category per month in the appropriate column. Then total it up at the bottom and multiply by six, adding 10 percent for emergencies. The total amount is what you must either have saved, have credit lines to, or must earn from your business immediately to keep yourself afloat for six months.

Personal Expenses.

APPROXIMATE COST PER MONTH   131.

Rent/mortgage . . . .

Utilities: HEATING, LIGHTING, ...

Local taxes, and Rates . . . .

Clothes . . . .

Food . . . .

Entertainment . . . .

Children's expenses . . . .

Medical . . . .   Add

Car or transport . . . .   10 percent
for emergencies

(Add others) . . . .   and multiply
x 6 months
to get your

TOTAL . . . .   grand total.

You may decide to budget a salary for yourself that will cover your personal expenses as part of your start-up costs. If the business can't support you totally at the beginning, I do recommend that you pay yourself a salary, however small, that will cover your Social Security payments and payroll tax.

That tip was one of the best bits of advice that my accountant gave me thirty years ago, when I first started my own business, and it's just as relevant today. Other than ensuring that you will receive all your government or state entitlements, it will give you a sense of self-appreciation.

Also, don't forget to budget enough money to cover your tax payments. Of course, start-ups don't pay capital gains tax until they start making a profit. But depending on your particular enterprise, country, and state, you may have to pay employees tax, Value Added Tax, sales tax, and other required payments, and it's essential to budget for them.

132.

"Don't give up your day job."

Some people manage to start their new enterprise while working full- or part-time at their current job. In any event, unless you've got some substantial savings, or don't already have a job to give up, don't give up your "day job" before you really have to. This is usually when you are sure of the viability of your enterprise and how to create it.

Salaries (including your own) and taxes are two items that must be figured into your overall business budget. At this point, you can start to prepare simple business budgets so that you can project the financial viability of your SEED enterprise.

EXERCISE: PREPARING YOUR BUSINESS BUDGETS

There are various budgets that need to be worked through before you can amalgamate them in your business plan. You should already have the information for most of these, and if you can't estimate your budgets for advertising, marketing, and public relations, you can add them after creating your marketing plan later in the Handbook, in Chapters Nine and Ten. The important thing is to create simple budgets for every aspect of your business.

Looking back to Chapter Six, you should have all the information together to calculate what you need to spend on both basic office essentials and the tools of your particular trade. From that information, create a list with approximate prices next to each item.

Budget: Basic Office Essentials.

ITEM	APPROXIMATE COST
Computer	. . . .
Printer	. . . .
Fax Machine	. . . .
Filing Cabinet	. . . .

133.

Budget: Tools of My Trade.

ITEM	APPROXIMATE COST

By now, you should have a pretty strong idea of where your business is going to be located and what you need to furnish it. You should have researched what to expect in the way of rent, local taxes, electricity, phones, etc. List these "location" items below—according to "monthly costs" or "one-time-only purchases"—and approximate their amounts.

Location Budget.

Monthly Costs

EXPENDITURE	AMOUNT
Rent	. . . .
Local business taxes and fees	. . . .
Electricity, gas, water	. . . .
Postage	. . . .
Telephones	. . . .

134.

One Time Only Purchases

Leasehold	. . . .
Decoration	. . . .
Furniture, etc.	. . . .
TOTAL	. . . .

If you're going to need such things as messenger or taxi services or delivery services (FedEx or UPS), don't forget to approximate these costs as well. These tend to be "hidden costs" because they're easy to forget about. Make a list now of all the areas of potential hidden costs that need to be calculated into your business plan. We've added a few of our own as suggestions:

Hidden Costs.

EXPENDITURE	PER ANNUM
Publications and periodicals	. . . .
Trade organization memberships	. . . .
Messengers, taxis	. . . .
Travel	. . . .
Printing, photocopying	. . . .

Now calculate the approximate amounts you will have to spend monthly on employee salaries (including your own). Once you hire a lawyer and an accountant, they will help you to determine how much to figure in for employee taxes and other required tax payments.

135.

Salaries and Taxes.

STAFF	AMOUNT

Finding Your Financial and Legal Team.

Then there are the nonstaff people costs—advisers such as accountants, lawyers, and other consultants. Your first order of business should be to find your team of financial and legal advisers. Personal recommendation is always the best way to find accountants and lawyers, so start asking your friends, family, and business associates who they use and if they'd be appropriate for a start-up business.

Start collecting phone numbers and make appointments with those advisers who sound the most suitable, checking that they don't charge for the first appointment. Remember that legal and financial advisers specialize, so make sure that whoever you select is appropriate for your particular enterprise. And don't ignore personal chemistry. You want whoever you work with to be sympathetic to your vision as well as patient and accessible.

Most lawyers, accountants, and financial advisers work on a per-hour basis, and the rates can vary immensely. Go through their costs carefully, checking on any hidden costs or expenses they may charge. The bigger their company and the more centrally located their office, the higher their fees usually are.

Try to find a small operation, which can give you the good advice you need at a price you can afford. Ask them how much time they estimate they'd have to spend on your business the first year, including setting up the legal structure, registering the name, creating a trademark if necessary, and all the other legal and financial needs you are going to have.

Work out what this will cost overall and add this to your budget below, together with the legal registration fees and taxes that they can tell you about. Also, ask your accountant to advise you as to whether or not you'll need to hire a bookkeeper.

Sometimes it makes more sense initially for you to look after your money yourself, with guidance from the professionals, and then look for a part-time bookkeeper once you're more established.

Taking a crash course on basic bookkeeping at a local evening college, or even a more general one on business management, would be a very good idea if you haven't had some practical financial experience in the past. I studied bookkeeping as part of my secretarial training more than thirty years ago and I found it essential when setting up my first agency.

136.

Another positive aspect of today's technology is that you can buy software for your computer that can do a lot of your bookkeeping for you. Either way, estimate the approximate charges, bearing in mind that in many places, particularly the United States, you can find a very inexpensive payroll service to work out staff wages, taxes, and Social Security. Your accountant will help you determine what interest rates for your bank loan might be so that you can figure that into your business plan.

Legal and Financial Costs.

EXPENDITURE	AMOUNT
Accountant	. . . .
Legal setting-up costs	. . . .
Bookkeeper, payroll service, computer bookkeeping program	. . . .
Bank loan fees and interest (see "Raising Your Initial Capital, pg. 108)	. . . .

137.

Finally, there are the costs of your products. If you intend to go into a service industry, you or your proposed partners or employees are the product, and various aspects of the service you wish to offer have to be calculated, many of them intangible. Your experience and talent, for example, have to be estimated out at current market costs, and you have to calculate what your time is worth by the hour or day.

If you are thinking of going into manufacturing products or retail, it gets more complicated. For example, if you are manufacturing, you'll need to add up your costs per item, which will of course have to include your other overheads, and then add on profit. The wholesale or retail price will vary according to what price you can charge for your product. To give you a guideline, most retailers double their wholesale costs as the markup for their retail prices. Most manufacturers, depending on the industry, add another fifty to eighty percent on their production costs to create their price.

This is where your research is essential. You need to visit shops and trade exhibitions to determine the prices you should be charging. If there is a strong design element in what you are making, you will be able to charge what you believe the market will stand. You'll soon find out if your price is right.

A silverware jewelry designer friend of mine from L.A. sells his highly original work in Japan for many times what the actual silver is worth, and yet the trendy Tokyo set literally queue around the block because of his exquisite designs—and because all the local rock stars wear them!

Now that you have some preliminary budgets prepared, copy them into your budget files or better still, put them on your computer, ready to be updated and inserted in your forthcoming business plan.

138. Raising Your Initial Capital.

Many of us have had wonderful ideas for a new business only to be stymied by the essential question, "But how do I come up with the initial investment?" The answer is clearly going to be different for each of you, according to how much you'll need. Perhaps you can fund yourself, or get help from family, spouse, or friends. Or maybe you will have to go to a financial institution to raise the money.

Financial institutions range from your local branch of a large commercial bank to small community banks to investment bankers and venture capitalists. And they will all need proof from you of your financial planning. For that matter, even your relatives will want to know the specifics of how you intend to initiate your business and turn a profit.

This is just one of the reasons why we will be emphasizing the importance of creating a business plan in Chapter Nine, to show whomever you're going to approach for money that your business concept is potentially profitable.

Selecting Your Bank.

If you have a good relationship with the bank you are already with, make an appointment to see the manager or loan officer and outline your general plans. See how he or she responds to your future needs, explaining that you would like to meet with her or him again once you have a written business plan in place. If you have a positive response, talk to them about their interest rates and see how flexible they are. Bear in mind that all interest rates and fees will be a major overhead for you to add on to your start-up costs.

Be prepared, though; banks in general are not very positive about lending money to women. My friend, New York communications strategist Nell Mellino, who created the "Take Your Daughters to Work" campaign with the Ms. Foundation, told me that the software used by banks all over the United States is developed by one private company in San Francisco.

As you well know if you've ever had to raise money, the questions on the bank loan forms, which spring from that ubiquitous software, are far more focused on your status as a single or married woman than on your potential to successfully run a business. Of course, this bias against women applies to banks around the world and not just in the United States.

Nell is currently launching a nonprofit organization code-named Broad Confidence in Women. It will give working women all over the United States the opportunity to collectively pool money—just five dollars a year—to create an independent source of capital for redistribution to women in the form of economic and technical education and small business loans.

This is a plan, which, I believe, would create value anywhere. It's similar to some of the best micro-credit programs currently operating in Asia, including that of SEWA—Self-Employed Women's Association—which has been running for more than thirty years in Northern India.

The women there have built their own bank, have group training for many areas of empowerment and enterprise, and their own insurance plan, despite growing up illiterate and among the poorest women in the land. They are the street vendors, the rag pickers, and the freelance construction workers, many married in their very early teens, bearing children while they are still children themselves, and considered the chattels of their husbands.

However, by working together and supporting each other, under the dynamic leadership of former trade unionist, lawyer, and Gandhi follower Ella Bhat, they have taken their lives and the lives of their children into their own hands and created value for themselves and their communities.

I have met Ella Bhat and heard her speak on several occasions, as well as visited SEWA headquarters in the Northern India city of Ahmedabad. I have been inspired and moved beyond words to see how these enterprising women, in the hundreds of thousands, have empowered themselves and each other.

As Nell gets her project off the ground, alongside other already existing micro-lending programs, we are going to see a shift in the traditional attitude of banks toward women. After all, at a time when women are the fastest growing group of new entrepreneurs, it doesn't make sense for banks to do otherwise.

In the meantime, make sure that you personally interview the bank officials responsible for loans at those banks from which you intend to borrow money. Find out what their attitudes toward women-owned businesses is, how flexible they are with regard to overdrafts, and how friendly they are. Make sure you get to meet as many of the decision-makers at your chosen bank as possible, and try, in this day of impersonality, to create some kind of personal relationships.

Borrowing money from a bank is never easy, and be prepared to have some of your own, or someone else's, collateral available. Try to avoid putting your house up as collateral, particularly if you have a young family. This was a near-fatal mistake I once made when starting a high-risk fashion shop with my ex-husband. Collateral can be in the form of shares, insurance policies, pension funds, jewelry, or art. Or someone close—parent or spouse—could guarantee your overdraft facilities or loan. Never risk more than you can afford to lose!

Personal Investors and Investing in Yourself.

Borrowing from a bank isn't the only way to get your business off the ground. Most of us know people who would be open to the idea of investing in our enterprise: perhaps the proverbial "rich uncle" who believes in you, or friends and relatives who also believe in you but may only be able to afford a modest investment.

If you are bringing in friends, lovers, and neighbors as financial partners, beware. Look at the relationship you have with each and decide firstly if you're even compatible enough with that person to be in business with them. Secondly, be aware that even the best of friends and lovers can fall out when it comes to money and business.

Do you want your parents or partner to be constantly on your back about their investment? If they do become investors, unless you want their professional involvement, make it very clear that you want complete autonomy. Also, always conduct your meetings in an organized and professional way. Make sure that they fully understand the risk they are taking and that they can afford to stand the loss, if anything goes wrong.

There are other ways to find investors outside your own circle, who might want to have some involvement with a business such as yours. Investment bankers, wealthy individuals, venture capitalists, and angel investor networks are all possibilities. There are trade organizations that you can find them through, or ask around for recommendations and introductions.

141.

This can be an expensive way to finance your business, though, where you may have to give away a large percentage of shares. However, if you need a lot of funding, you should explore all possible avenues.

Speak also to your national and regional small business agencies, which can recommend different financing routes, including themselves. Some of these provide loans for women- and minority-owned businesses or can point you in the direction of those who do. There are also women and community banks in certain places, which are obviously more sympathetic toward women-owned businesses. Again, a lot of funding-source research for this can be done on the Net. If your proposed business is a nonprofit or community service one, you can also search the Net for foundation or government grants.

The type of arrangements you could make with your potential investors vary between some form of partnership, where the business shares are distributed (don't give away more than forty-nine percent if you want to keep control), to a more straight forward return of the loan, either short or long term, plus interest rates.

Ways to Save Money.

While planning your budgets, be creative about ways to save money. I've listed several ways for you to cut costs and once you get going, you'll need to keep an eye out for others.

- Interns or students are often available for work experience and can save you the cost of one full-time staff member.

- Take advantage of the many inexpensive telephone services.

- Collect your air miles wherever you can.

- Check out if your trade associations offer joint cooperative purchasing strategies.

- Research reasonable leasing terms.

- Always search the Net for bargains.

- Plan your credit terms, whether buying or selling, as advantageously as possible, so that your cash will flow.

142.

Community Currency.

Even as we in the First World are entering the twenty-first century, we are beginning to see the value in placing ethics, trust, and community support as priorities. Local programs are inspiring many of us to seek ways to integrate creative economic ideas into our mainstream, profit-orientated economy. As you consider how you might finance your new SEED enterprise, perhaps you will be inspired to use aspects of the barter and trade systems. The following stories will provide some role modeling.

- In Ithaca, New York, they have printed their own money since 1991. Called Ithaca Hours, the printed bills are accepted by three hundred seventy shops, businesses, and service providers within a twenty-mile radius of the city. One Ithaca Hour is redeemable for one hour of basic work or ten dollars.

According to Paul Glover, who created the Ithaca Hours program, "A ten-dollar bill comes to town, shakes a few hands, and leaves. An Ithaca Hour stays around." In other words, Ithaca Hours encourage people to shop at locally owned businesses rather than to frequent chain stores owned by distant corporations. In fact, printed on the bills are the words: "Ithaca Hours stimulate local businesses by recycling our wealth locally. Hours are backed by real capital; our skills, our time, our tools."

There are now more than forty other U.S. communities with their own currency, including the community of artists, retailers, professionals, and service providers on the Mendocino Coast in North California. Their currency is coincidentally called SEED, standing in this instance for Self-Sufficient Ecological Economic Development.

- The LETSystem—Local Exchange and Trading System—is a network of people who agree to trade in a particular way. It is founded on the principle that everyone is fairly rewarded for their work. The system was developed in British Columbia in the late seventies by an academic named David Weston, and was taken around the world from the early eighties by Scots-Canadian Michael Linton.

Michael Linton brought LETS to Britain in the mid-eighties, and by the recession in 1992 there were forty trading systems operating in towns and cities all over the country. Check the back of the Handbook to see if there is a LETSystem near you. Or contact an existing one to find out how to start a LETSystem yourself.

- Womanshare—a "co-operative skill bank" for women—was started in New York's Upper West Side in the early nineties by Jane Wilson and Diana McCourt. Womanshare groups are now starting all over the United States, where the participants not only exchange skills, but share "joyous living," as their principles put it.

The scheme has now come to the U.K. Organized by Let's Link U.K., a group of 150 Asian women living in Leicester have called their scheme Narri Lets. They gather together to support and empower each other, much like they do naturally back home with their extended families and communities.

At the very least, why not test the idea of bartering by offering some form of exchange to suppliers while setting up your enterprise? I've often helped with P.R. advice in return for design work or other necessary tools of my trade and as Hazel Henderson says, it is a win-win situation.

Bartering is the exchange of goods and services for other goods and services without the use of cash or community currency. This can be done on an informal basis, as I've done, or by forming a network with a group of others for whom an arrangement like this would work.

- Barter Business Network.com is easy to find on the Internet, and they promise they can give you access to creating business relationships that fit your company's needs. In fact, rather like a marriage broker, they'll get you together with the appropriate barter partner, although this is still primarily in the United States.

According to them, sixty percent of Fortune 500 companies, the biggest corporations in the world, are currently involved in some type of barter.

I am sure that barter on a community level, as well as through the Internet, will be one of the most important changes in regard to economy and small businesses in the future.

My friend Peggy Horan, who lives further up the California coast at Big Sur, told me how she and her partner were midwives for years in the region, paid in food and natural products.

At Orchard School, a private community school in Aptos, Northern California, the parents barter the school fees by giving their secretarial services, teaching specialized skills, or maintaining the wonderful grounds and little farm enjoyed by the children.

145.

Controlling Your Money.

Money is a very complicated subject, which like so many of our chapters, really deserves a book on its own. However, I think the most important thing to remember is to always own money; never let money own you. It is just energy and there to be exchanged and used.

Some of the most "needy" people I've met, who always seem to be worried that they don't have enough, are the very rich. And some of the most generous and hospitable people I know have very small incomes. It really is a question of balance—sustainable balance.

Claudia Duenas is an L.A.–based rock singer, freelance operations manager, wise young goddess, and friend, who advises a number of small entrepreneurial businesses, including mine. She believes that doing unto others as you would have done to yourself, remaining faithful to your financial principles, and putting other people's needs first whenever possible ("It comes back to you many times over," she says) are the crucial things to keep in mind.

Claudia certainly encourages me to stand up for my principles with my clients in my communications business, with regard to financial arrangements and legalities. And I have seen how our clients respect us more because we clearly state our financial principles and stick to them.

Claudia pragmatically advises new entrepreneurs to stay on top of their budgets, and to remember to set aside funds for health insurance, a retirement plan, and tax-free investments.

Manifest Abundance.

146.

I have always believed that any of us can manifest abundance in our lives. I practiced a form of Japanese Buddhism for many years, where I chanted every day to manifest specific things in my life. I definitely manifested many things, but I became so focused and controlling that I sometimes got things I thought I wanted but didn't need. That old chestnut! I forgot how to be open to change and stay with my inner flow.

Positive thinking, focus, and intention can produce just about anything—as long as you are prepared to let go and leave the final work to the greatest Creator of all.

Now, at this point in the program, go to your sacred place in nature or in front of your altar for some grounded prayers to develop your own powerful powers of manifestation. Repeat the following affirmation, or one of your own, during your quiet times, while you are putting the financial aspect of your garden design in place.

"I offer gratitude to the great Creator, for the wonderful abundance in the world about me.

I am ready to manifest and receive the necessary means to enable me to expand my life through my SEED enterprise."

chapter

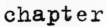

8

Creating
your
Seed
Community

THE SEED HANDBOOK

Where you decide whom you want in or near your SEED garden.

Do you want to start your enterprise on your own or with active partners? Will you need staff? Which are the networks that will nurture and support you? How can you be part of a community and still work on your own?

We humans are tribal beings living in a separatist society. Our basic need is for connection. More and more of us throughout the world are living in big cities with the anonymity that large urban populations are prone to. We've lost the extended families and tribal living that are part of our real nature, and which we can only now find in rural villages in developing countries.

Business relationships replace the extended family for many people, and our colleagues and work contacts can often be pivotal figures in our lives. I'm sure that this is one of the reasons I've started a new business, despite having a warm, loving family and lots of friends.

150.

After selling my first agency, it took a lot of getting used to for me to work on my own again. I had enjoyed the tribal feeling of working with a lot of people who'd become close personal friends. I also enjoy leading a team through the creative process, where we all participate in developing the ideas and seeing what works.

Those of you who want to leave the corporate world to start your own business may find it difficult at first to work on your own. Being responsible for yourself and your business is very different than working at a job where you have the backup of colleagues, bosses, and group decisions.

If you want to start an enterprise and have been at home concentrating on your family, you'll probably find it easier to work on your own. Being solely responsible for your family's schedule, budgets, and general organization is, as we said at the beginning of the Handbook, good experience for being an independent entrepreneur.

But if you're already part of a small entrepreneurial business and want to break away to do your own thing, you know that if you work with the right team, with all the chemistry going, it can be great fun.

And even if your enterprise is essentially a one-woman operation, there's no reason why you have to work entirely on your own. There are various ways of linking up with others, which will add value to your business and make the process of working far more enjoyable.

In this chapter, we're going to talk about a number of ways to include other people in your SEED business—so that it expands to become part of a SEED community.

SEED Partners.

The reason for taking on a partner in your business can be, as we've already shown, purely financial. Such partners are basically investors, who are rarely involved in the day-to-day running of the company.

But there is often just as much practical reasoning for forming a different kind of partnership. Your gifts and talents may need balancing with another person's skills. And you may really enjoy the joint responsibility.

When deciding who would make the ideal partner, think very carefully about approaching close friends, family, and spouses. There's so much existing baggage that comes into a business partnership when the personalities involved already have a close personal relationship, that it puts extra pressure on all the way around. Balanced partnerships work better when the relationship is strictly business.

Business partners can fall out really badly, especially if they are your romantic partners, too. My ex-husband and I worked pretty well together, when he joined my agency some years after I founded it. It was the marriage that suffered though, with all our conversations at home centering on the business. I remember our children sitting in the back of our car on several occasions, asking us to stop talking "shop." If only I'd listened, I suspect my marriage might have been a more intimate experience.

When initially negotiating with your business partner, you have to decide how much ownership you each have. If you are investing the same amount of money and have equal responsibilities and skills in running the business, then it would presumably be fair for an equal division of shares.

But for those of you who recognize your strong leadership qualities, an equal partner may not be comfortable for you, with every decision always having to be discussed in detail by both of you. Bear in mind that if the share division is fifty-fifty, it's stalemate if you have a disagreement.

The important thing to remember when creating a balanced partnership is that whatever the personal ties are with your partner, there needs to be clarity between you, with an acknowledged division of responsibilities.

You should work out from the beginning how you would pass on the shares if the partnership didn't work out. You must also be clear about whether there is joint signing of checks, who has the authority to order supplies, and who would be the outside mediator, should there be a dispute.

This may all sound rather negative, but it's better to be prepared for the worst. Partnerships in business are like any relationships—nothing is guaranteed forever.

152.

EXERCISE: DO YOU WANT TO BE A LONE SEED OR ARE YOU WILLING TO SHARE THE GARDEN

Go to your quiet SEED place and check in with your inner voice, as well as your logical brain. Find out if you want to undertake this enterprise completely on your own or whether you'd like company.

Answer these simple questions in order to focus your mind on this issue:

• Do you prefer your own company to being with others?

• Do you consider yourself an independent person?

• Do you prefer to make decisions on your own or do you like to share the process?

• Are you open about your financial situation or would you rather keep such matters to yourself?

• Do you consider yourself a team player?

• Do you need your space?

Not neglect
my personal
Relationships,
loved ones
and

friends in
any way

Notice how you've answered, and it'll be quite clear to you whether you'd work well with a business partner, or whether you'd prefer to be the sole proprietor.

SEED Staff.

Employing others to work for you is clearly another aspect of creating your SEED community, but only when you can afford it. Think about your potential workload and check out your budget. Do you think you can do everything that is necessary to start your business off on your own or will you need help?

If you intend to open a retail business of some kind, it is pretty certain that you'll need help, although an extra sales assistant could be part-time to begin with. You'll also need a part-time bookkeeper, unless you're really bookkeeping-savvy, which few entrepreneurs are.

If you're planning a service business, it's possible that you'll need office help as well as other personnel backing you up. Whether you decide to employ others now or later, there are certain things you may want to bear in mind regarding your arrangements.

Firstly, you have to remember that you're not the only one wanting to work in the new, feminine way. Your team, too, will be looking to join an enterprise that reflects their inner values and allows them to express their creativity to the fullest.

The feminine way to do business is not the old-style autocratic way of treating staff, where the decision process is kept shrouded in mystery at the head of the hierarchical company structure; where employees are expected to work in airless, small spaces; and where there is no consideration for employees' personal lives.

An open environment, both physically and creatively, in which all your team can contribute as a group, where they feel appreciated for their work and respected as individuals, is more important to employees, according to most polls these days, than high pay and perks.

A company's philosophy toward social responsibility is also considered crucial to many potential employees. According to research done by Prince Charles' Business in the Community organization based in London, companies that are open and positive about their commitment to giving back to society receive a far higher standard of graduate applications.

Of course, finding the right team is often a case of trial and error. Word of mouth using all your contacts is often the best way, so put out the word and let people know the sort of person you'd like to work with.

What about employing friends and family? In some cases, this may work, but as in partnerships, only if your working relationship is clear and professional. Overfamiliarity can confuse the relationship and not end well, from a personal as well as business point of view.

My son and daughter, now in their early twenties, receive rave reviews from anyone they've ever worked for since they've started their own careers. But anytime they've reluctantly agreed to help me, dragging their heels all the way despite the money, it has not proved a great success for any of us.

Checklist for Interviewing Potential SEED Staff.

Before you begin the interview process, make a list of what you're looking for in a person, not only on a professional basis, but also in terms of their "people" skills. In addition to being efficient and well qualified for the job, are they upbeat and friendly? Are they good listeners? Do they seem to be sympathetic to the vision you have for your business?

Here are some tips for interviewing potential staff:

- Observe their body language and their style of dress. Do they seem comfortable with themselves, and does their appearance seem to fit in with the business you envision?

- Ask them about their personal interests as well as their professional skills.

- Let them do most of the talking.

- Ask them about their last job and why they left.

- Notice how they refer to their past employers.

- Make sure they have realistic expectations about the job that you're offering.

- Ask them for their reasons why they want the job.

- Find out what their long-term life vision is—do they see themselves going for a trip around the world, moving to another country, writing a novel? If you're planning to train them, balance your investment with the time you think they'll want to stay with you—although nothing is guaranteed in any kind of relationship!

If you can't find the right people by networking, try advertising in the local or national newspapers. I've always found that placing a classified ad in the newspaper is more effective than using trade press, and employment agency fees can be very expensive if you're a start-up business.

Be sure about whether you really need full-time or part-time staff. Once you employ someone full-time, you're responsible for paying their taxes and other contributions, holiday pay, and sickness benefits. Are you ready for that responsibility yet?

156.

Creating a SEED Team Feeling.

It's important for the members of your team to feel their own passion for the company as well as a sense of ownership. With my new agency, Globalfusion, I am structuring a share-ownership scheme as well as a variety of empowering opportunities for the bright young women who have helped me found and build the company. I encourage everyone to be involved in the decision-making regarding how we will grow as a business as well as contribute to the values by which we want to work.

We start off our working day by meeting around the kitchen table, lighting a candle, and holding hands for a blessing for the day, and sharing of what's going on for us individually —as they do at the Findhorn Foundation.

We then discuss the day's work plans and suggest how we'll handle the various situations that are going on. I've made it very clear that I see the business's future very much in their hands, as well as mine, and that they are my successors. We jointly discuss the

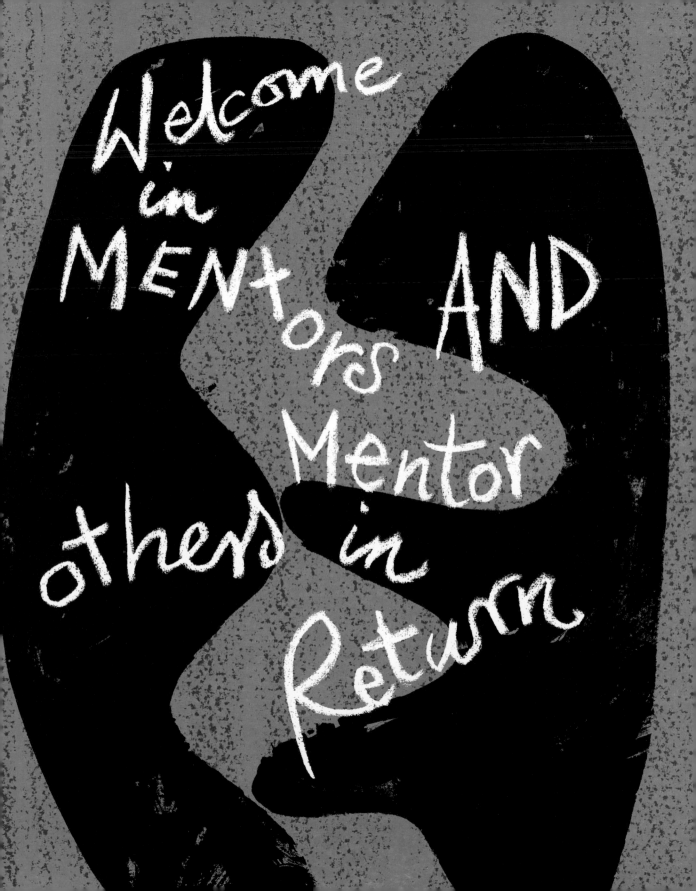

additions we want to make to the team and the work skills we need to bring in.

My team trusts me, and I trust them. There is love and empathy between us, and we are, as a group, constantly striving to create the feminine way in our business. We accept our individual strengths and weaknesses and support each other as much as possible in the course of our very busy day. We're interdependent, and, I like to think, growing organically into an organism that is based on values, mutual respect, integrity, and professional brilliance. I also believe strongly that we should all have a personal life, holidays, time off when we need it, and pleasant working conditions.

We work out of my home office, and I always make sure the cupboards and fridge are full of goodies to be shared by everyone. I treat everyone the way I want to be treated myself, and I know that it's appreciated. Of course, it's taken awhile to get to this point of having a staff who work well together and share the SEED values. A few early members of the team didn't work out, and I've learned over the years the importance of letting go with grace when the chemistry is wrong. The right people are often just around the corner.

158.

Research the market salaries for these positions, and if you think you can afford it, add the necessary staff members to your budget.

BOOKKEEPER

OFFICE MANAGER

SECRETARY/PERSONAL ASSISTANT

SHOP MANAGER

SHOP ASSISTANT

RECEPTIONIST

TECHNOLOGY EXPERT

DESIGNER

159.

Networking and Mutual Mentoring.

Creating a SEED community involves not only the possibility of choosing an appropriate partner or partners and putting together a qualified and values-oriented staff, it also entails reaching out to potential customers, suppliers, neighborhood and national organizations, and even competitors. The alliances and friendships you build can come from a number of different synergetic areas.

Networking and mutual mentoring with individuals from many organizations and sources has always come naturally to me, and has been a key reason for the success of my businesses.

Of course, there is limited time to network when you are starting a new business, but you have to consider it a crucial part of twenty-first-century business technique. You will learn so much, bring in new business, and make some great friends, many who—have gone through the same experiences and growing pains as you have or will.

Groups to which you could reach out could include communal and local co-operatives and partnership networks; professional trade associations; women's and ethnic minorities' business organizations; socially responsible, environmental, and sustainable business networks; and the local chamber of commerce and other semi-official business groups.

By being in contact with others in this way, you will be weaving a web of energy and connections that will help sustain and nurture you and your business, as well as allow you to be in a position to nurture and inspire others.

I have been a member of, as well as public relations adviser to, a number of professional trade associations over the years, predominantly in the fashion and entertainment industries, where I've specialized. This has made more sense for me than participating in my own profession's association.

160.

I've also been a founder, member, or associate of a variety of British, American, and international professional women's networks over the years, to whom I have spoken on many occasions. This has enabled me to enjoy a role of mentor and sharer of experiences and information, which of course I am always happy to do.

However, I've always considered that I have received the most valuable input and contacts for my own professional and personal growth from a variety of different types of sources. Among them are, for example, Social Venture Network—a group of socially responsible entrepreneurs primarily from the United States and Europe—and the Brahma Kumaris, the only women-led spiritual organization in the world, whose constant focus on spiritual values and service to others in daily life has inspired me along my path toward developing SEED.

Both these groups hold international conferences several times a year, where they bring together visionaries from the academic, business, political, environmental, and development arenas to dialogue on a variety of subjects that affect the future of this planet.

My main realization from attending these conferences, and others pertinent to our future, is that it is time for the world's business community to take responsibility for improving

look AT difficult situations from ALL Perspectives

society and the environment, instead of exploiting them. There needs to be a just and healthy, holistic integration of all cultures and countries and environments in our world, and for that to happen we must each transform the way we operate our businesses.

Although I've always considered myself to be socially responsible as an individual, exposure to an extended community of entrepreneurs and visionaries through these associations has taught me how to apply my values and create change through my own businesses in practical ways.

Networking is how I first met the inspirational bundle of energy, Anita Roddick, founder of The Body Shop, who, together with her husband, Gordon, were two of the original members of Social Venture Network, along with my friend Josh Mailman and Ben Cohen of Ben & Jerry's ice cream.

Anita has for many years generously given her time to a variety of business, educational, and women's networks, and speaks at large and small meetings all over the world. She inspires all who come into contact with her with stories of her own experiences, good and bad, as well as her intelligent and articulate vision of how we can improve the world we live in.

But I'm sure Anita would be the first to admit that she's received a tremendous amount back from her networking, in the form of ideas and information which she's used to create breakthroughs at The Body Shop. I was delighted to see that as part of her current communication campaign to support hemp farmers, she has a hemp leaf with the words "Sow the Seeds of Change" at the bottom of her fax paper. A great, synergetic message for SEED entrepreneurs.

Social Venture Network members not only meet at exciting conferences and exchange experiences, they also support each other's businesses, knowing that everyone is coming from their integrity with the same set of values. They trust each other and have an investor's circle that has, on occasion, financed one another's projects. In the United States, they are now creating their own organic food wholesale cooperative, where a number of them are involved in putting the S.V.N. principles of social change through business into practical application.

They are an unusual organization, as is their sister network, Business for Social Responsibility, which is currently only in the States. However, its large membership is open to overseas companies, and they, too, hold regular conferences where they meet each other, hear inspiring speakers, and exchange information.

Research the women's and other business networks that you're most interested in and get yourself on the mailing lists so that you can attend meetings or conferences held locally. You'll not only meet other likeminded souls and business contacts, you'll also be creating opportunities to grow your SEED community and to improve the environment in which we all live and work.

Some Necessary Networking Tips.

- Always carry business cards and don't be shy about distributing them.
- At the end of the day write on the back of any cards that you receive, where you met the person and any important notes about them.
- Follow up new contacts with e-mail or faxes.
- Send people you meet samples of your work, if appropriate.
- Listen to and be interested in others.
- Be generous with your information.
- Be open to networking at unusual locations. Could be the hairdresser's, the beach, or at a family wedding.

163.

Community Networks and SEED Centers.

If the type of enterprise you have chosen to create really is a one-woman or -man show, but you still crave being part of a local community in which people help each other, why not create your own network?

Think of ten people you know, or know of, living in your area who are all involved in different, but synergetic, fields of work. One could be in media, one in retail, one an academic, one an economist, one in technology, and so on.

Invite them all to a meal, and explain that each of you could share knowledge of what is happening in your own specific field, which would benefit you all.

Try it once, see if it works, and suggest you meet every month or so at each other's homes to exchange information that will help all of you in your work.

Alternatively, you may appreciate being part of a group of other small start-ups in your area, who can share experiences and problems, and even do joint purchasing.

Either way, when you set up your own local business network where members can exchange information, goods, and services with each other, you create a mutually beneficial SEED community. For example, why not agree to write marketing material for the local printers in return for them printing yours for free or at a discount? Find out where you're in a position to give local businesses the benefit of your products or services, in return for them helping you.

Link your various contacts together, so they can work with each other in the same way. Give your partnership network a name and expand it, if appropriate. Hold meetings at which you have speakers and exchange information.

You could even take the idea of community networking further and consider sharing space. I've been developing the idea for some time of SEED Centers, where a group of enterprising women and men, committed to the same principles, share a building and overheads with each other. An old school, empty warehouse, or even a large house would be ideal, where there is room to breathe and even have a garden.

Of course, you'd have to sort out the legalities as to whether you'd have to jointly share the lease or whether one of you takes it on. Just ensure that responsibility is clearly stated and the arrangement is financially secure for everyone.

When you're creating a SEED community of this sort, it's important, too, to bring a group together that can service each other as well as their normal business customers. A perfect mix of professionals and businesses might be a lawyer, accountant, childcare center, general store, caterer, dry cleaner, marketing consultant, graphic designer, and secretarial service, all sharing facilities such as joint reception, cafe, quiet room, office support, and equipment.

The SEED Center could be the perfect solution for solo entrepreneurs who don't find it convenient to work from home or prefer to work within a community.

SEED Support Groups.

Another way to get support—emotional and otherwise—is to encourage a group of friends who have also been talking about opening their own business to work through the Handbook with you. If you can't find anyone who wants to start a group, you can link in with the SEED Web site—seedfusion.com—and connect up with people. Meet every two weeks, and start the meeting with a lit candle and quiet meditation, followed by group sharing. Learn from each other's experiences, and support and mentor each other.

Whether you meet in person or on-line, remember that you have automatically become a member of the SEED community by reading this Handbook and participating in the SEED program. Through our road shows, on-line chat rooms, and conferences, you'll meet other SEED entrepreneurs, with whom you can exchange experiences, discover SEED solutions, and find and give encouragement.

166.

And don't forget—you'll need the support of your personal community, too. Keep your family and friends abreast of your vision and ask for their patience and help while you're giving birth to your dream.

MEDITATION TO BUILD YOUR SEED COMMUNITY

Go to your quiet place and put out the positive intention to attract the right people into your life to help you build your SEED community.

Repeat this meditation aloud during your morning and evening quiet time over the next few days.

"I ask the great Creator to attract the right people into my life to help me build my SEED garden. I put out my intention to treat my SEED community in the way that I wish to be treated myself, with respect, value, and love."

Sketching the Garden Plan

Where you structure your business plan, project your dreams into reality, and draw a complete picture of your SEED enterprise.

chapter

9.

Now that you've done your research—on yourself and your prospective business—and have thought and felt your SEED enterprise into being, it's time to put all the material you've gathered into a more formalized plan, while at the same time ensuring that your business philosophy is also in place.

Your business plan is the left brain's version of your SEED Vision poster. Even though your business plan will be essential when talking to a banker or potential investor, it is first and foremost for you. It is where you can see if all the pieces of the puzzle fit together and whether your enterprise will be sustainable financially, as well as representative of your values.

This is the time in the SEED program when you write your mission statement, set your specific goals, bring your budgets and financial projections together, decide on an action time line, and plan your marketing strategy.

Who's going to buy your products or services, and how are you going to reach them? You need to decide on a communication program to reach your market, and bring it in line with the rest of your business plan.

There are many business courses and books that set out the logistics of designing a basic business plan, but there are certain common, sense rules to follow. One of the biggest mistakes you can make is to create a heavy tome of a plan, which is difficult to read and boring to look at.

We live in an immediate world, and the most impressive business plans that I've seen—and I've seen many different kinds—are those that are kept succinct and easy to read, written with the passion and energy of the entrepreneurs whose businesses are being described.

Writing the plan, which involves examining all the different aspects of what will make your business viable, will give you the opportunity to make any last-minute changes and adjustments before you launch your new SEED enterprise.

The Parts of the Plan.

The executive summary at the beginning of your business plan explains your SEED Vision and is what will excite prospective readers. The rest of the document will demonstrate the validity of your concept.

Generally the items that constitute a business plan should include the following:

- a list of contents
- an executive summary
- values and mission statement (SEED option)
- a list of the management team
- your goals
- your products
- marketing strategy (including competition)
- action plan/timeline
- financial strategy (including risk elements)

As you think about writing each of these sections of your business plan, don't panic, or, as I often can when faced with this kind of task, glaze over. The SEED business plan should be as easy to write as it is easy to read; it's simply a matter of putting the necessary points over in your own style.

I have at this point got to come clean—although I'm a great planner with my creative ideas, I've never had to raise money from investors for my businesses and have never written a formal business plan, either.

But like so many other so-called coincidences with my own business development while writing this book, I'm now at a point in my businesses where I need to write a business plan for both, to enhance my management strategy.

Somewhat to my own surprise, I am finding the process of writing a business plan an extremely helpful way of clearing my own thoughts and making me be far more focused about the route I want to take forward.

My original concept for SEED, long before I had a name or a book, was to start a global network of women entrepreneurs from all different backgrounds, who could share information and knowledge. The main emphasis was on education and training, through personal empowerment, and the tools were to be a combination of books, live events, audio-visual aids, and, of course, the Internet.

The way I envisioned my concept was a circle, a bit like an orange, divided into segments, each one autonomous but interdependent with the other parts.

As I was looking at our wonderful SEED logo, designed by Ann Field for the cover of the Handbook, I realized that the circle I used to constantly draw to surround a brief description of my business concept could be the center of the SEED daisy. And the petals could each contain a word to describe an element of my plan.

If this floral diagram works for me, why not you? It's a feminine way of making the writing of your business plan less of a chore and more of an organic experience.

EXERCISE: FILLING OUT YOUR SEED DAISY BUSINESS PLAN OUTLINE

Before you get into the detailed workings of your plan, why not take some quiet time and sit in front of your sacred SEED space? Let the numerous voices in your head, with their messages about money, time, marketing, and business teams, all float out to the universe, while you ask the Creator for guidance and clarity to bring all the aspects of your SEED enterprise into simple perspective.

Once you feel clear, as a fun way of visualizing how your plan will work, fill in the SEED daisy. Write a brief description of your enterprise in the center of the flower. Then write a word or two in each petal, describing a different quality that you want to see represented in your business plan. These may include your values or some practical aspect of the business such as "well managed," "well located," "motivated," or "innovative."

You don't have to use the daisy; use any visual design that resonates with you. When my friend, intuitive, and astrologer Michelle Bernhardt decided she needed a business plan to raise funding for "Inner World," her products and event-focused enterprise, she used the visual imagery of the solar system to focus her thinking.

MY SEED BUSINESS PLAN

Write On!

Now that you've used the SEED daisy as a framework for thinking through the different elements of your enterprise, it's time to flesh them out, remembering to keep your written descriptions brief but inclusive.

The following general guidelines will help you as you write your description of each section of your SEED business plan.

What's in a Name?

The very first page of your plan should always be the cover sheet, featuring the company name, a logo if you have one, and your contact details—address, phone, fax, and e-mail—plus the words "private and confidential."

By now, you should have an idea of what you want to call your enterprise. It may be as simple as using your own name, particularly if you are going into the service area, such as marketing services.

Alternatively, you may have been inspired by your visioning to think of a word or phrase that resonates with your personality or sense of humor, and at the same time is appropriate for the business.

There are specialist companies all over the world that get paid a lot of money to come up with a new brand name for the corporations that can afford to pay them. This is unlikely to be the route you'll be taking at this point, but I'm sure you are a creative entrepreneur with your own imaginative ideas. So hire yourself! Put your creativity to work in order to find the right name for your enterprise.

I believe names, like most words, have tremendous power and create an energy that can have a dynamic effect on your enterprise.

EXERCISE: CHOOSING A NAME FOR YOUR BUSINESS

Go back to your SEED vision poster and scrapbook. Look at the words you wrote down or cut out and make a list here of the ones that could work as a name for your business. Make the name easy for people to remember and pronounce. Consider whether or not the name will work well in the industry you're entering, and make sure that it hasn't been overused.

Possible names for my SEED enterprise

....

....

....

....

....

....

....

....

....

175.

Once you've made your list, set it aside for a few days, take some quiet meditation time to think about your choices, and then draw up a short list of three names to research for availability.

The easiest way to check on name usage these days, is of course, the ubiquitous Internet. You'll get immediate feedback as to whether or not the name you're thinking of is already overused. It's also very possible that one day you'll want your own Web site, so don't choose a name that you can't register because someone else has the same one.

Once you've settled on a name, register it as a Web site name as soon as possible. It's easy and inexpensive and will protect you, even if you don't use it as such for a while.

San Francisco–based Web site producer Frances Stack offered to check out SEED for me when we first met. She found literally thousands of different seed Web sites, whether ending in ".com" or anything else. We finally decided on seedfusion.com as our unique Web site address, fitting in neatly with the Globalfusion Web site, created by the brilliant international designer Brett Wickens (married, fortunately for Globalfusion, to my colleague Coralie Langston-Jones).

Frances told me that you just go to www.networksolutions.com, then click on the "Need Help to Start?" icon. From that point you should follow the easy steps provided to determine if the name you're considering is available. When you have established that your business name is not taken, you may then proceed to register it in a quick and easy registration process, which will cost you seventy dollars or approximately forty-five pounds for the first two years of service.

You may also reserve a Web address, which can be used to send e-mail, build a Web site or hold it "just in case." There are specialist services that will manage your Web address on their secure servers very inexpensively.

Trademarking your company name and logo can be an expensive process, but according to specialist international trademark lawyer Donna Rubelman it's particularly important for any business launching a national or international consumer brand or product. She told me, "Your company name is your business signature and should be protected as much as possible."

"However, if you're starting a business in the technical or services area, it's not so important to trademark," she added. "And if you're doing any kind of enterprise in your local area, such as a small retail outlet, it's really not necessary. Just ask your lawyer to check that you're not picking a name that is already trademarked by someone else and which you can get sued for using—like McDonald's."

You should also check phone books, trade association lists, and any other available information to see if anyone else is using the same (or a similar) name in the same type of business in those countries in which you'll be doing business.

The rules for registering business names vary from state to state and country to country. You need to check any choice you make with your lawyer or with your local registration office. Your local small business advisory bureau will be able to direct you to the appropriate organization.

Using Your Own Name.

Of course, an alternative to selecting a "brand" name for your company is to use your own.

178.

Using my own name for my original P.R. agency had its advantages and disadvantages. It turned my name into a well-known brand, which was useful in terms of giving me the opportunity to speak at industry events, and getting lots of personal publicity, which reflected positively on the business.

On the other hand, it made the agency look too much like a one-woman brand, with clients feeling neglected if they didn't get my personal attention, despite the business having over fifty well-qualified staff members.

This time around I've created brand names for my businesses—Globalfusion and SEED— in the hopes that they will grow from the combined energy of the team members working with me.

My businesses reflect more than just me as their founder. They also represent the ideas, values, hard work, and commitment of my colleagues, who are empowered to make their own decisions and take ownership as my successors.

The literal meanings of both names also have a direct effect on how the businesses are viewed both internally and externally.

Globalfusion presents a picture of the international, dynamic fusing of culture, lifestyle, and communication. SEED creates a feeling of an organic, nurturing, feminine energy.

I relate all of this to you so that you'll stay conscious of all the positives and negatives of giving your enterprise your own name, and of the advantages you can create by using innovative, synergetic words as a business name.

The summary should include the big picture of your enterprise idea and why it will work. Current market trends and how your enterprise fits into them should be included.

Some business books advise you to put your financial requirements, should you need a loan, into the summary, alongside when and how you'll pay it back. However, I think it's best to explain the creative concept first and leave the financial details to last.

By now, you should be able to verbally describe your dream enterprise to the significant people in your life. Before you put pen to paper, why not practice explaining the concept of your business, who it's aimed at, and why it will work, initially to your friends and family?

Verbally explain the plans for your SEED enterprise as clearly and succinctly as you can, observing if your audience easily understands what you're saying. Ask them to give you feedback on your idea and presentation, and without being too sensitive, take their comments on board. Then adapt your written summary accordingly.

You may find it easier to write your executive summary after you've written the various other items that make up the business plan document, summarizing a little from each. Personally, I like putting down the big picture first, because that inspires me. Then, after I've written the rest, I check to make sure that I haven't left anything out of my initial summary.

Values and Mission Statement.

Although mission statements, setting out the company's values as well as aims, weren't an essential part of any of the business plans I came across in my research, when I was forming Globalfusion, I developed mine before I did anything else.

I was full of many different ideas when I decided to start a new business in the United States. Not having a business partner or senior management team to talk things over with at that time, I worked with independent "creative manager and mentor" Raymond Davi, who gave me some terrific feedback and structure for my vision.

One of the first things that I developed with Ray was getting my mission statement clear, not only to include the big picture of my new business, but to incorporate my values into the basic structure.

I had made various notes before my first session with Ray. By talking them through with him, and using his method of putting all key thoughts onto large poster-size paper with bright-colored pens, all around the room, I was able to put my statement together in a way that read well and resonated with my inner thoughts. Here's a copy of my mission statement to show what I mean:

180.

GLOBALFUSION: MISSION AND VALUES STATEMENT

MISSION

- Globalfusion is dedicated to bringing creative communications, which embody twenty-first-century consumer values and lifestyles, to business. Globalfusion calls this innovative process "New Marketing."

VALUES

- Globalfusion is passionately committed to creating open communication through the values of integrity, personal responsibility, sustainability, and authenticity.

MISSION OBJECTIVES

- Globalfusion connects people, ideas, businesses, and non profit organizations to create cutting-edge values-led communication strategy, both domestically and internationally.

- Using the resources of multi-media communications, we will establish partnerships between media, technology business, and society, which, as well as being commercially viable, will contribute in a creative and positive way to the marketplace.

- Globalfusion is committed to the principles of ethical communication and values-led leadership.

181.

EXERCISE: WRITING YOUR OWN MISSION STATEMENT

Why not take a stab at writing your own values and mission statement? Look back to Chapter Five where you wrote down the values you most want present in your SEED enterprise. Using this list, write a paragraph describing how those values fit into the mission for your business. Your mission statement isn't as detailed as an executive summary; rather, it's a brief declaration of your creative concept and vision.

....

....

....

....

If you're having trouble writing your paragraph, start putting some sentences together, and when you feel they are starting to represent what you want to say, write them, as Ray Davi suggests, on big flip chart paper with bright-colored pens. Put them in a readable order and leave them up on the wall for a while.

I think every company should have a values statement, particularly as a constant reminder to the internal team. When I visited Women.com recently, I was immediately attracted to their values statement, hanging in the reception area of their Northern California head offices. Before I'd even met anyone from their company, I already had a good idea of the type of people I was there to meet.

SEED Team.

So that you and your potential investors can assess the strength of your team, write a paragraph or two about your own professional background and that of your full-time colleagues, advisers, and members of your board of directors, if you should have them.

In addition, the role of each team member should be defined. If there are any glaring gaps with regard to skills and abilities, they will soon become apparent to you as you write. You should ensure that your team includes a leader, a visionary, a financial expert, a product developer, a marketer, and a manager. Although these are often the same person in a small entrepreneurial business, try to name at least a few people besides yourself to lend credibility.

Ask your accountant and legal adviser if they object to being named as part of your team. Who else do you know who is an expert in areas where you are not? Would they be prepared to give you some advice at times? Would they be the people you would like to ask to join you as members of your board of directors or advisory board further down the line?

Most business plans have gaps on their management team, particularly in the areas of marketing, advertising, or public relations, which can be added later. You're not going to have the full team in place for a while, so visualize members of the team whom you would like to join you during the first year and add their roles in the respective areas on your timeline. (See p. 187 on creating your SEED timeline.)

I've allowed my name to be used on other people's business plans in the past, when I've believed in their project, and have found that it doesn't necessarily follow that I'll be involved once the business has been formed. You're not married for life to the people named on your business plan, but compiling this list is a good start toward creating your ongoing team.

You should end up with at least four people named on your plan as the management team. These people should ideally cover the areas of management, finance, product or service design, and marketing. Remember, too, that you should always try to surround yourself with individuals whose business strengths are your weaknesses. Do what you do well and delegate the rest.

Background, Goals, and Products.

You need to write a page on each of the above subjects. The background of the company should cover when the business was founded, who the directors are, even if you've covered this on other pages, and any other facts which you may think are appropriate.

The goal of your business is basically your vision—do you want to be the biggest and the best at whatever you want to do? Do you intend to be the leading e-commerce company, selling environmentally friendly stationery, or the creator of a mail-order company, selling textiles and jewelry from global artisans? What is your big picture and what are your goals in getting there?

Finally, of course, you need to explain your products or services in a clear understandable way, on their own page. State why they are different from anything else already on the market and how you intend to distribute or retail them.

Marketing.

What are you selling and to whom?

The section of your business plan that covers marketing should precisely define your products or services, and your customers. You may think you know exactly what these aspects of your enterprise consist of, but a fresh, close examination of what you're selling and to whom is always beneficial.

Perhaps your vision is of a health food shop, but are you really certain what types of food you're going to sell? Will you include fresh fruit and vegetables? What about bread and dairy products? Will you also sell vitamins and cosmetics? Is there a shop in your area that's, already selling health food? If so, how is yours going to be different? Who is your store specifically aimed at?

You need to include a full explanation of your offer together with the market you are aiming at. Give your assessment of your market, whether it's growing or stagnant, and what competition is out there. Get out all your research on your product or service, which you collected earlier on in the SEED program, and use it to write this section of your business plan. Then define your specific customer, incorporating all the appropriate lifestyle information about them.

If you're thinking of opening an exclusive women's spa, for example, you could be aiming your business at the following potential customers:

Women aged between twenty-five and forty-five, mostly professional workers with disposable income, a high rent or mortgage, who eat out three times a week. They tend to join clubs, want to feel special, and read *Vogue*, *Marie Claire*, and *Elle*. They don't watch much TV but do surf the Net. They spend a lot of money on fashion and beauty, read books, and like to think they are organic. They are mostly single, and earn upward of thirty-five thousand dollars or pounds a year.

In a more general sense, they are a growing market of independent working women, who are not impressed with old-fashioned, aspirational advertising, are very health orientated, don't wear heavy makeup, and exercise at least twice a week.

184.

This is all hypothetical of course. But it gives you an idea of how to analyze your potential client or customer and her lifestyle. The more specific and accurate your analysis, the more impressed with your thoroughness and expertise your potential investors will be. It will also help you tremendously when strategizing your communication plan.

Marketing Strategy.

There are many ways of communicating a business's message to its market. You may have some very original ideas for doing so. But there are certain marketing basics to keep in mind when developing your plan.

- **DIRECT MAIL**, using promotional material or a personal letter, is one approach that is most common in business-to-business communication.

- **LOCATION** and **SHOP WINDOWS** are often the most effective marketing tools you have if you are in retail, although good publicity and advertising will help, if you have the budget or contacts.

- **TRADE EXHIBITIONS** are important, if you're in manufacturing or wholesale, as part of developing a brand awareness campaign.

- **NETWORKING** in both your community and industry is important to establish your company's reputation.

- **PUBLICITY** and **ADVERTISING**, whether you're selling a product or service to the consumer or to the business sector, are always important. You can oversee these efforts yourself or use a consultant. We're going to cover these areas in some depth in Chapter Ten, and then you can decide which route to take.

- **WEBSITE** telling your company's story and linking into as many other relevant Web sites as you can get to is more important than ever. Include an aspect of e-commerce in your business plan, explaining where you will sell your product or service on the Internet, if not for right now, certainly for the future. Web sites are expensive to design unless you or a close friend is a cyber wizard. You can get quoted anything from a few thousand dollars or pounds up to half a million to design one. Find yourself a wizard, who can help you create a dynamite site for a reasonable price.

186.

We're going to examine other ways to launch your enterprise in the final chapter, but for now think through the ideal marketing plan to get to your audience.

As with any aspect of business, there is no mystery to marketing. Having studied, analyzed, and thought about your potential customer, you should be clear about who you are trying to sell to by now. Just think about what would encourage someone to come to you for your product or service. What might they read or see that would motivate or impress them?

And what is the most that you can afford to budget for your marketing costs? Ask your accountant or financial adviser for some help in determining this. You'll need an approximate figure for the final section of your business plan—the financial strategy.

Timelines - Personal and Professional.

In addition to helping me refine my mission statement, Ray Davi also made some other very helpful suggestions in guiding me with my business timeline. A business timeline is essentially an action plan, with each activity aimed at being achieved within a certain timeframe.

Ray talked me through all the things I needed to do for both Globalfusion and SEED, and put this year-long "to do" list into realistic three-month time periods.

It's hard to plan for every activity too far in advance. Looking back, I can see how much other work also needed to be done that we didn't initially include on the timeline. However, this early plan covered some major activities and gave me a great kick-start.

To give you an insight into how to prepare your own timeline, here is my first year's planned activity for SEED, which you may want to refer to as a model.

187.

SEED Timeline 1999.

JANUARY–MARCH, 1999

- structure legal and financial parameters
- trademark SEED in appropriate markets
- secure Web site names
- confirm agreements with publishers
- create separate timeline for book production

APRIL–JUNE 1999

- prepare initial cover design for book
- start planning Web site concept and partners
- research case histories in United States, U.K., and elsewhere

- network with women's groups

- begin writing initial business plan

- open SEED bank account

JULY–SEPTEMBER 1999

- finish book

- plan road shows for 2000

- negotiate road show sponsors and media partners

OCTOBER–DECEMBER 1999

- start P.R. program for 2000 launch

- open office

- secure sponsorships for road shows

- get initial Web site up and working

- hire initial staff/team

- write treatment for SEED TV series on women entrepreneurs

EXERCISE: CREATE YOUR TIMELINE AND ACTION PLAN

If your initial funding is in place, you probably have a launch date in mind for your enterprise. It's obviously got to work in context with the type of business you're opening. For example, if you're starting a shop specializing in "back-to-school" recycled stationery, you're not going to want to open in the middle of the school year. On the other hand, if you're opening a healing center, any time is a good time.

Regardless of whether or not you have your funding in place, write down an intelligent estimate as to when you're likely to open your SEED enterprise. Make a list of all the things you need to do within the coming year to get your business launched and off the ground.

Then, using Ray Davi's simple but effective method, write down the four quarterly periods, starting from next month, onto large pieces of paper with colored pens. Allocate each action to a realistic time period and when you're happy that it flows comfortably, put the information into your computer as part of your plan.

Financial Strategy.

The last section of your business plan requires that you turn all your budgets and projections into cash flow and spread sheets, which clearly show how and when you're going to make some money.

If you feel you have the knowledge and experience to do this yourself, then go ahead. But if you want to make certain that this important area is based on firm ground, ask your financial adviser or accountant to do the figure work for you. This is an expert's job, and by now you should have your financial expert on board.

Some basic financial guidelines:

1. Keep your potential growth in mind.

2. Do not commit to personally investing any more than you can afford.

3. Be prepared to cut some carefully considered corners.

4. Don't hesitate to pull in some favors to get your SEED enterprise up and running.

5. Always set enough aside for a "rainy" day.

MEDITATION: GRATITUDE FOR UNDERSTANDING
THE WHOLE PICTURE

Have you covered everything you want to say about your business in your business plan? Do you now have a clear picture of what you need to make your SEED garden a reality?

It is time to shape your plans into a firm foundation for your future SEED enterprise.

Go to your sacred place in nature or in front of your SEED altar and repeat aloud during your morning and evening quiet time:

"I give thanks to the Universe for helping me understand how to plan my garden so that it will fully bloom."

Where you plan your
celebrations on becoming
a SEEDpreneur and
invite all your clients
and customers to join
you in your vision.

The Garden Party

Like a garden, the seeds of your business have taken root, pushed through the soil, and are ready to bloom. You just need to make sure that your invitations have gone out and that your garden is ready to be seen by all the guests at the garden party.

It's launch time, and your plans are reaching fruition. It's time for action—you should have your logo in place, your finances worked out, your workplace and tools set up, and your business cards at the ready.

In Chapter Nine we talked about the outline of your marketing strategy. In this chapter you'll decide on the route you are going to take to build up an awareness campaign that will attract the customers and clients that your business requires.

194.

Now that your new enterprise is nearly a reality, you may find that your biggest fears are beginning to surface. After all, you're about to go public, expose your dreams to the world, and find out if they're going to work.

It's perfectly normal to feel nervous about failure, but if you've done your research and preplanning thoroughly, your confidence level should remain high. The difference between an idea and a success story is "perseverance." Stay firm but flexible, understanding that your idea can always be adjusted and improved upon.

Just prior to launch is the time when creative blocks and fatigue can set in. Just lean into them, take your own time, and ground yourself by entering your quiet time and space. As you move into this last exciting phase of creating your SEED enterprise, ask your higher self to work with the Universe in keeping your dreams and energy focused.

If need be, go back to the prayer at the end of Chapter Two and repeat it aloud, in your morning and evening quiet time, until you are ready to acknowledge your courage in getting thus far with your enterprise.

Planning Your Launch Program.

There is no one perfect way to launch a new business. I have successfully launched and promoted more businesses than even I can remember over the past thirty years, and each situation is unique.

It is impossible to supply you each with a tailor-made marketing and launch program, as much as I'd like to. There are many different methods and techniques that can be adopted, depending on your type of enterprise and, of course, with whom you're trying to communicate.

If your target market is the business community, you're not really interested in creating widespread consumer awareness. In the main, such awareness applies to technical goods or services. Reputation is of the ultimate importance in the business sector, but that has to be earned.

In the meantime, it is necessary to communicate the information that your business exists, exactly what it offers as a product or a service, where it can be found, and, if appropriate, an idea of charges.

If you've already worked in this sector, you'll know many of the people in the industry who are your target market. Equally, if you've done your research thoroughly, you'll have a database of the individuals you need to connect with.

You could create some corporate literature, if your business is large enough to warrant it, but I wouldn't recommend anything too costly at this stage of the business. Printing an expensive brochure or some other permanent form of communication doesn't give you the flexibility of changing things around later.

A better idea is to send a personally written letter, perhaps accompanied by a small appropriate gift, to your "hit list" of potential clients or customers. The letter should be written in a professionally friendly way about what it is you want to sell, and why it's an interesting proposition for him or her.

In this chapter we'll be discussing a range of launch ideas. Feel free to pick and use the ones that suit your particular SEED enterprise.

Attracting Press Coverage.

Obtaining print publicity in your specialist trade or local media is, of course, an immense advantage when opening your business. Apart from the awareness that printed publicity can bring when it originally appears, distributing photocopies of the article in an appropriate way can encourage new business and have a tremendous effect for years to follow. The endorsement of your product by any form of print media—because it's the easiest to reproduce—without advertising (if you can get it) is an extremely important part of the marketing mix.

The way to encourage a feature article in the appropriate journal can be easy if, like any situation, you know the right people or can be introduced to them—often the role of a public relations agency.

However, if you don't know any journalists in the relevant media and can't afford a public relations agency—and it's an expensive business—you'll need to research the specific journalists and publications that could write about your company as a news story.

EXERCISE: COMPILING A PRESS LIST

It's important to start putting together a press list, where you record the publications, contact details, and names of the relevant journalists who influence the thinking of your target market—and this applies to both business and consumer products.

Always include the specialist writers for your national newspapers and magazines, even if you think they won't be interested in you yet. Keep in touch with them from the beginning, and let their interest in you grow as your business does.

Don't restrict your press list to just print publications. Add to your list all other forms of media—TV, radio, Internet, community newsletters, high school newspapers, and local and national business newsletters—that may influence your market, and get hold of a copy of or watch or listen to every appropriate publication, program, or Web site. Remember to bring your list up to date as often as possible.

Once you've got your list together, write a friendly—but not overly familiar—personal letter to the particular journalist, introducing yourself and your company. Keep it chatty and to the point, noting why you think this would make a good story for them. Attach a more formalized press release, written on your company letterhead, describing all the details of your business in the third person, with a relevant quote from you, perhaps emphasizing the values behind your business.

EXERCISE: HOW TO WRITE A PRESS RELEASE

Of course, everyone has their own style of writing, but there are certain standard points you'll need to get across in your press release. Mostly, they're a matter of common sense.

- First of all, write a strong heading at the top of the page, getting at the core of your story without giving it all away. For example, if you're going to open an exotic flower shop, perhaps the heading could read "SCENTSATIONAL BLOOMS," or if you're starting a marketing consultancy for women entrepreneurs, it could read "WHAT WOMEN WANT."

- Start the body of the release with the essence of your story, stated briefly, including why it is interesting or unique. Remember that you're writing a press release, not an editorial, and don't overembellish or exaggerate—it can make a journalist cringe.

- Use the next two or three paragraphs to tell the details of your story—i.e., what, when, where, and how. Include a quote from you on the overall vision for your business somewhere in the first half of the release, to set the tone.

- Finish off the release, which should never be more than two pages of 8 1/2" x 11" paper, and preferably less, with some background on you and your business concept, and always add your contact details.

- Always leave yourself a little time after writing it and before sending it out, to reread it and see if it needs improving.

Now, write your own press release, describing your SEED enterprise in the third person, in an objective but positive way. Include all the aspects of your business that make it appealing and unique, and write the release in your own sharp, effective style.

The Corporate Profile and Business Fact Sheet.

Additional materials you could include in your press pack are a business fact sheet or a corporate profile. To help you formulate your own, here is an example of each.

The first is a business fact sheet that is part of the very professional press kit I received from top British TV producer and creator of children's programs, including the Teletubbies, Anne Wood.

RAGDOLL PRODUCTIONS (UK) LTD

KEY FACTS

• *The internationally acclaimed producer of children's television series, Ragdoll Productions (UK) Ltd was founded by Anne Wood in 1984 with the ethos that "Ragdoll Works For Children."*

• *Since then, Ragdoll has produced more than one thousand programs aimed at Pre-School viewers and has developed a successful market for complementary merchandise. The programs introduce early skills and ideas about literacy, numbers, science, and relationships.*

• *The much-loved titles Rosie and Jim, Tots TV, Brum, and Open A Door have been joined by Teletubbies. This multi-million-pound series has been made for the BBC and sold to fifty-nine broadcasters covering one hundred twenty territories in forty-six countries including the United States. It has been translated into twenty-one languages. Awards include Best Pre-School Programmed at the 1998 Children's BAFTA, and Grand Prize at the twenty-fourth Japan Prize International Educational Program Contest in Tokyo. This brings the total number of awards for Ragdoll programs to twenty.*

• *Ragdoll is based in Stratford upon Avon. It has a unique shop where half of the space is given over to creative and imaginative play, allowing children to explore replicas of Rosie and Jim's Ragdoll boat, see themselves on the screen through the windows of a lifelike version of the Tots TV cottage, play in a childsize version of the Teletubbies' Tubbytronic Superdome, and have a ride on Brum. This allows Anne Wood and her team to learn from the children in an environment devoted to their series' characters.*

- All Ragdoll's programs are live action, filmed on location, with production bases in Stratford upon Avon and at Pinewood.

- Ragdoll is also the name of a full size fifty-foot canal boat used in the filming of Rosie and Jim.

- In Tots TV, which has won two consecutive BAFTA Awards, the cottage is a real one—built to a small, children's scale. The series is shown daily in the United States.

- Brum, the little yellow car, is a real car—custom-made for the BBC series.

- It takes an average of fifteen hours' creative work to produce one minute of a Ragdoll television program.

- Ragdoll researches each program carefully with the collaboration of its unique network of consultants, nursery teachers, parents, and carers, among others.

Sometimes it's necessary to tailor your business profile to suit the needs of the business or financial media. Here's a particularly readable corporate profile that I received from the hugely successful women's Internet portal, iVillage.com.

CORPORATE PROFILE

iVillage.com

Within iVillage.com, there is a community for every interest, and links to more than fifty experts, thousands of message boards, and constant access to a volunteer network of one thousand plus "community leaders."

Nancy Evans (former president and publisher, Doubleday; creator of Family Life *magazine) and Candice Carpenter (former president of Q2 and Time Life Video), founded iVillage.com in 1995. Their mission: to humanize cyberspace. Nancy and Candice have built the best communities on-line, by developing a safe place where women can talk to other women about everyday life issues. iVillage.com doesn't dictate what its members should talk about, it programs according to what its members are talking about.*

From signing on to find a recipe for dinner, to getting support for coping with the crisis of infertility, women come to iVillage.com in search of camaraderie, and to handle everything from more trivial to extremely serious concerns.

If you have relevant photographs available of either yourself or your product, include them in either print form or transparencies, together with the press release, fact sheet, or corporate profile and enclose all your information in an attractive folder with your letter on top. Soon press kits will be delivered electronically or on a disc, but for the time being, investing in a professional-looking printed press kit is worth every penny or cent.

Following Up.

Follow up your letter and press release with a personal phone call. Invite the journalist to lunch or to meet you so you can explain your story in person and, if you have any, show your products. Sound enthusiastic without being too pushy or aggressive.

If whomever you're calling is too busy to get together with you, and most will be, then offer to pop by their office to meet. If they make it clear that they are too busy right now to even see you in their office, which may or may not be a brush-off, disengage with grace, still using the opportunity to explain your story as one that will fit in with their editorial pages.

There is an art to this like any other form of successful communication. Don't bother a journalist until you are ready and prepared to tell your story in a succinct, clear way. You should be able to relate it in sixty seconds or less. When you're next watching the news on TV, notice how the presenters talk in brief "soundbites"—you need to learn to do the same when necessary.

Again ... Networking.

Often the most effective way to attract your initial customers is to create contacts, through networking, who are in a position to send you business your way, or become clients themselves.

talk SLOWLY

but think quickly

I started both my P.R. and communication agencies with one client already on board. When starting a client-led service business, it's always a question, to use a still-useful cliche, of what comes first, the chicken or the egg.

In the case of Lynne Franks P.R., it was my first client, fashion designer Katharine Hamnett, who actually suggested that I start my own P.R. business, offering to come on board as my first client. I had originally met Katharine through a trade exhibition, where I was assisting on the P.R. and she was selling her first collection.

We immediately connected, despite coming from different types of backgrounds—she was a diplomat's daughter from Cheltenham Ladies College, a very proper English boarding school, who'd then attended the very hip St. Martin's College of Art in London's Covent Garden.

I was a Jewish butcher's daughter from North London, who'd attended a state grammar school and left school at sixteen. I'd had a stab at journalism, after working for a teenage sixties magazine, *Petticoat*, and a mail order company, and had drifted into a career in the emerging area of fashion public relations, which was servicing a whole new area of sixties trendy fashion companies.

Despite our differences, Katharine and I became friends. We were the same age, with the same idealism and the same passion for new, exciting ideas to work on. Through our networking, we not only recommended business to one another, we also started a friendship and we also entered into a business relationship which has survived on and off for thirty years, and is still going strong.

202.

Cause-Related Marketing.

Some of the most successful, international media coverage that Katharine ever received was based on her big slogan T-shirts in the early eighties. She came up with the idea of affecting public opinion through "message" fashion after I took her to a Buddhist exhibition called "Choose Life."

Using such phrases on her over-sized T-shirts as "World Peace Now," "Save the Whale," and "58% Want Pershings Out," referring to the American nuclear weapons then on British soil, Katharine was a huge success and created an entire new medium for social activism. She wore the "Pershings" T-shirt when photographed with Mrs. Thatcher during a government reception at Ten Downing Street, which resulted in an enormous amount of international publicity for her as well as her message.

I publicized the message T-shirts as fast as Katharine could design them, and they were reproduced in fashion magazines all over the world. The idea got copied by the successful British pop band Frankie Goes to Hollywood, plus many other musicians, and did much to inspire the thinking behind the world-changing Live Aid music fund-raiser, organized by Bob Geldorf in the mid-eighties.

Katharine did not design the T-shirts because she wanted to create publicity for her new and already successful business, but because she felt, rightly, that it was an effective way to get certain environmental and political messages through to the public.

However, she did get an extremely high profile by designing them, which encouraged her reputation as an intelligent, thinking woman, designing wonderful clothes for other intelligent people. She also benefited in ways which are now recognized as major boosts to any company's image: celebrity endorsement and association with social causes which will benefit others. And all for the right reasons.

Another inspiring case in point is that of Jo Fairley, a successful journalist as well as owner of Green and Black's, the British organic chocolate company, which launched her Maya Gold brand in 1995 in conjunction with the U.K.-based Fair Trade Foundation (FtF). By buying the chocolate from Mayan farmers in Belize, Central America, directly through the grower's organization, Jo and her entrepreneurial husband and partner, Craig Sams, were able to offer the growers a unique long-term contract and a far better price than many of the larger corporations.

Their conditions of trade were within the strict guidelines and conditions established by the Fair Trade Foundation, an independent certification body supported by some of the major British charitable organizations such as Christian Aid, Oxfam, the National Federation of Women's Institutes, and others.

After visiting Belize to satisfy themselves on the trading arrangements, FtF organized a promotion for fair deal trade to coincide with the launch of the chocolate. They arranged for twenty thousand young British churchgoers to participate in a run across the U.K., lasting for twelve weeks, with the aim of raising awareness of fair trade issues and to try to persuade individual supermarket buyers in the towns they stopped at to stock fair trade products. The young Methodists handed out thousands of leaflets and samples. The BBC covered the story on three different news bulletins and even sent a film crew to Belize to photograph the local children eating the chocolate.

Because of their policy of fair deal trading and close links with the Third World, Green and Black's received an enormous amount of support from religious communities—even to the extent that local clergymen were holding tastings and calling up supermarket buyers. There was also a great deal of additional national press coverage, and the chocolate is now stocked at all the major supermarket chains and health food stores in the U.K., as well as being exported to Europe, Japan, and the Unted.States. The chocolate also happens to be very delicious and is wrapped in distinctive packaging.

At this point, I would also like to acknowledge and honor the late Linda McCartney, whose personal commitment to vegetarianism and passion for cooking and family inspired her own entrepreneurial undertaking.

Despite her own already busy life, playing and touring with husband, Paul's, band, being a publicly acclaimed photographer, and mother of four with responsibility for the family's large Sussex farm, Linda decided that there was more that she needed to do with her life. Her strong love of animals, and belief that the public should be educated to understand how delicious vegetarian food can be, inspired her to create a range of widely available packaged foods.

In partnership with frozen food giant Findus, Linda created her own delicious array of frozen, easy-to-prepare vegetarian food that became some of the best-selling items of their kind in most supermarkets across the U.K. She promoted them widely, exposing herself to all kinds of media coverage that she really didn't need. Her unique way of starting a business to promote her message is further proof of how one's personal values can determine the communications strategy of a new enterprise.

There are many other success stories of businesses from all over the world that use their communications resources to put over positive social messages from their founders.

Using your social message or company values as part of your promotional platform means you can put over your beliefs and sometimes your political message, help affect public consciousness, and create awareness for your products at the same time. Cause-related marketing has become an accepted, if not leading, part of the mix for many major consumer brands, and should be the aim of all entrepreneurs.

Katharine Hamnett

Anita Roddick

Linda McCartney

Hot Cookies on the Radio: Coming Up with Creative Launch Ideas.

The way a business reflects its social values isn't always a matter of "big causes." Simply making your customers smile is, in itself, a "good cause"—and a wise marketing strategy. Debbie Fields, the energetic founder of Mrs. Field's Cookies, told me that since she was a child she has always believed that her primary role in life is to make people smile. This "mission"—together with her love of cookies —is what underlies the passion that Debbie brought to the opening of her very first cookie shop when she was only twenty years old. And she still feels that passion to this day.

When a customer leaves any of her shops, it is more important to Debbie that he or she feels happy and is smiling, both from the product and the service, than any profit she's got in her till.

I launched and promoted Debbie's business twelve years ago, when she came to the U.K.

206.

One of the most successful aspects of the launch I did for Debbie in London typifies the sort of creativity SEED entrepreneurs can easily employ. I sent boxes of hot Mrs. Fields' Cookies to all the early morning radio presenters in the areas where Debbie was opening stores, and saw that they were delivered personally just as the broadcasters were about to go on air or when they were already in the studio.

It worked perfectly, was not expensive, and nearly all of the DJs who received them raved about them *on the air* during their busy morning radio shows.

Radio is a very under-appreciated medium. Most stations have high audiences, many of them women, and it's much easier to target your market through radio than it is through television. See if you can persuade your local station to interview you—but don't contact them unless you're sure that your story will work for them. Listen to the show first!

It's far more difficult to publicize your business via TV, although television is obviously an ideal medium for publicity. TV personalities are not nearly as accessible as their radio counterparts, and they tend to use the stories they are given by their producers. Your best bet is to contact the show's producer or researchers with an idea, which would promote your business and would work well on their show.

You could either come up with a "story" that includes your new business and is appropriate for their show, or make a convincing "pitch" for why an interview with you would be of particular interest to their viewers.

Community Synergy.

If you are opening any kind of local shop or service, it is pretty essential for you to create some kind of inexpensive leaflet or flier.

Remembering how important your graphics and name are, work on creating an eye-catching piece of information that will interest your potential client or customer.

Distribute your fliers everywhere you can. Without being overly invasive, get your leaflets into any venue where your potential customer might visit. They could include libraries, community centers, business centers, doctor's and dentist's waiting rooms, childcare nurseries and baby clinics, schools and colleges, health spas, and gyms. Think of all the places that your potential customers may spend their time and would have the time to positively read some information about your new business.

EXERCISE: WHERE ARE YOUR SYNERGETIC BUSINESSES AND OUTLETS?

Make a list of all the places in your community where you could arrange to distribute your business announcement, leaflet, or brochure.

....

....

....

....

....

Shops and other local businesses are generally very happy to cooperate, particularly if you return the favor by doing joint promotions. For example, together you can offer customers a combined discount or freebie. If you're advertising in a local newspaper, you might offer everyone who comes into your hair salon and spends more than forty dollars or pounds a good discount at the local fashion store. You could split the cost of the advertisement and draw potential customers into both outlets.

Shop Windows, Photo Opportunities, Sponsorships, and Freebies.

There are many creative ways to launch and publicize a new business and it's often a question of combining the tools you have at hand with a clever or quirky idea that will attract the attention of both the press and the public.

If you have a shop window, remember that it is the best form of advertising you have. If you're not good at creating an interesting—and newsworthy—window yourself, ask around until you find someone who is. Remember that your very first "launch" window should be something special. Approach it like a work of art.

Sometimes, the simplest ideas can have the greatest effect. For example, I've used live people as shop window mannequins when I've opened shops for clients in the past. Try and come up with an original idea that will bring attention to your store either inside your shop window or in front of your door.

210.

Even if you don't have a shop window, if your idea is visually unusual, it may make a good news photograph for your local newspaper. Try and come up with a stunt that could get your business message across while creating an exciting photo opportunity.

If you're planning a dog walking agency, for instance, borrow every dog you can find of all shapes and sizes, have them all on leads, and contact the local press to come and photograph you, walking all twenty of them down the main street of your town.

If you are starting a cake business, bake the biggest cake you can and deliver it to the children's ward of the local hospital. Tell the local papers that this is how you're celebrating the opening of your new business—another win-win situation.

Why not rent a huge billboard at a prime spot near your business and get it painted by students from the local college with your launch message? Then make sure that the local media know about it. Sponsoring an appropriate local event is another socially conscious way to advertise your launch.

If you're opening a vitamin shop, see if you can sponsor the local women's sports event or city marathon. If you're selling gardening equipment, become a sponsor of the local gardening show. Although sponsorships can be very expensive, find a way to make this launch idea fit your marketing budget—and you'll gain name recognition as well as community goodwill.

You could also consider giving freebies out at community affairs such as farmers' markets, village fairs, school fund-raisers, or even friends' dinner parties.

"Introductory offers" can also bring in first-time clients. If you're offering a service like a massage or manicure, why not offer introductory rates when you first start out? Advertise your offer for a short-term only, but invest in giving a generous initial discount.

Don't Forget the Announcements,

Now that you've completed all the SEED preparations to launch your new enterprise—envisioning, research, creation of your team, budgets, and marketing strategies—don't forget to let the world know that you're open for business. Or at least your particular part of the world. Make sure that everyone who is on your database of contacts, which you've been building up since you began your SEEDpreneurship, receives something that tells them you've set up shop. Whether it's an attractively designed postcard or a miniature sample of your goods, reach out to your community and announce that your enterprise now exists.

There are many imaginative ways to launch your business to its intended market. By trial and error you'll discover which techniques work best for you. Remember to be flexible enough with your marketing plan so that you don't spend all your budget before you find out which of your strategies gives your business the greatest boost.

Launch Party.

One last big decision before opening your doors is whether or not to hold a launch party. There are many reasons not to, and again I speak from experience. It can be costly and most of all messy, which is a pain when you've just redecorated and are opening to the public the next day.

I've experienced being down on my knees, cleaning cake off the floor when my fashion shop, Mrs. Howie, opened its doors in the mid-seventies. I had a party attended by London's trendiest media and "glitteratti" customers. We got a strong vibe out in the fashion world, received good press coverage, and piqued the guests' curiosity to come back and shop.

But I think I was the only person who didn't enjoy the party, because I had to make sure that everyone was happy and nothing was getting too ruined. If you can handle the stress, and make intelligent decisions about not serving red wine, not allowing smoking, or serving anything creamy, then go for it.

This is where your friendly celebrities come in handy. If you know or have access to any local or national well-known faces, ask them to your launch, explaining that you will be inviting the press.

If they are good friends, they won't mind being seen cutting a ribbon, smashing a bottle of champagne on the doorpost, or admiring your goods. It's part of the game and will ensure you some good exposure.

212.

So it's time for your garden party. You've told everybody you can possibly think of about your SEED enterprise and now you're finally ready to cut the ribbon on your special garden and invite everyone in.

But first you should return to your special SEED sacred place and invite in your most important guest. It's time to acknowledge that the Great Creator of All Things in Nature and in Life will be at the center of your party.

Commit to continue to experience your quiet times in front of your altar or place in nature, where you can ground your ideas, hear your inner voice, and let go of your stress.

214.

MEDITATION: PLANTING THE SEEDS OF MY FUTURE

Repeat aloud the following affirmation, or use your own words, as you prepare the final stages of the launch of your SEED enterprise.

"I am ready to introduce my dream to the world and make it a reality. I give thanks to the great Creator for partnering with me to make my ideal garden, through which I commit to planting the seeds of my values, principles, and joy."

So good–bye for now, and God bless. I feel as if I know
you, and have been talking to a friend all through this book.
I send you my love and good wishes for a successful SEED
enterprise. Remember to enjoy what you're doing and to
have a joyful, whole life.

See you in the garden,

Lynne x

LYNNE

PHOTO: JOHNNY ROZSA

Seed Books

Women's Ventures Women' Visions, 29 Inspiring Stories From Women Who Started Their Own Businesses, by **Shoshana Alexander**, *1997, The Crossing Press, Freedom, California*

The Feminine Face of God, The Unfolding of the Sacred in Women, by **Sherry Ruth Anderson and Patricia Hopkins**, *1991, Bantam Books, U.S.*

When The Canary Stops Singing, Women's Perspectives on Transforming Business, edited by **Pat Barrentine**, *1993, Berrett-Koehler Publishers, Inc., San Francisco*

The Right Brain, A new understanding of the unconscious mind and its creative powers, by **Thomas R. Blakeslee**, *1980, MacMillan, London*

Funny Money, In Search of Alternative Cash, by **David Boyle**, *1999, HarperCollins Publishers, London*

Wings of Soul, Emerging Your Spiritual Identity, The World and Wisdom of Dadi Janki, by **Brahma Kumaris Information Services**, *Health Communications Inc*

Real Power, Business Lessons from the Tao Te Ching, by **James A. Autry and Stephen Mitchell**, *1998, Nicholas Brealey Publishing Ltd., U.K.*

Seven Secrets of Successful Women, by **Donna L. Brooks and Lynn Brooks**, *1997, McGraw-Hill, U.S.*

The Artist's Way at Work, Riding the Dragon, by **Mark Bryan with Julia Cameron and Catherine Allen**, *1998, William Morrow and Company, Inc., New York*

Embracing Victory, How Women Can Compete Joyously, Compassionately, and Successfully in the Workplace and On the Playing Field, by **Mariah Burton Nelson**, *1998, Avon Books, Inc., U.S.*

The Artist's Way, A Spiritual Path to Higher Creativity, by **Julia Cameron**, *1992, Tarcher Putnam, New York*

Business Capital for Women, An Essential Handbook for Entrepreneurs, by **Emily Card and Adam Miller**, *1996, MacMillan, New York*

Fusion Leadership, Unlocking the Subtle Forces that Change People and Organizations, by **Richard L. Daft and Robert H. Lengel**, *1998, Berrett-Koehler Publishers, Inc., San Francisco*

Springboard Women's Development Workbook, by **Liz Willis and Jenny Daisley**, *1993, Hawthorne Press, London*

The Executive Mystic, Psychic Power Tools for Success, by **Barrie Dolnick**, *1998, HarperCollinsPublishers, New York*

Secrets of Self-Employment, by **Sarah and Paul Edwards**, *1991, Jeremy P. Tarcher/Putnam Books, New York*

The Best Home Businesses for the 90's, by **Paul and Sarah Edwards**, *1991, Jeremy P. Tarcher/Putnam Books, New York*

The Enterprising Woman, by **Mari Florence**, *1997, Warner Books, New York*

Learn To Relax, by **Mike George**, *1998, Duncan Baird Publishers*

When Money Isn't Enough, How Women are Finding the Soul of Success, by **Connie Glaser and Barbara Smalley**, *1999, Time Warner Audio Books, U.S.*

No More Frogs to Kiss: 99 Ways to Give Economic Power to Girls, by **Jolene Godfrey**, *1995, Harper Collins*

Twenty Secrets to Independence, by **Jolene Godfrey**, *2000, St. Martins Press*

A **Handmade Garden**, A Planner for Growing Flowers, Herbs and Specialty Gardens, by **Jean Haley**, *1998, Galison, New York*

The Hungry Spirit, Beyond Capitalism, A Quest for Purpose in the Modern World, by **Charles Handy**, *1997, Random House, London*

The Age of Unreason, by **Charles Handy**, *1989, 1991, Arrow Books Ltd., London*

The Ecology of Commerce, A Declaration of Sustainability, by **Paul Hawken**, *1993, HarperBusiness, San Francisco*

The Web of Inclusion, by **Sally Helgesen**, *1995, Currency/Doubleday, New York*

The Politics of the Solar Age: Alternatives to Economics, by **Hazel Henderson**, *Doubleday, Anchor*

Redefining Wealth and Progress, by **Hazel Henderson,** edited with Frank Bracho, *TOES Books/Bootstrap Press*

Building a Win-Win World, Life Beyond Global Economic Warfare, by **Hazel Henderson,** *1996, Berrett-Koehler Publishers, Inc., San Francisco*

Paradigm In Progress, Life Beyond Economics, by **Hazel Henderson,** *1991, Berrett-Koehler Publishers, Inc., San Francisco*

Creating Alternative Futures, The End of Economics, by **Hazel Henderson,** *1996, Kumarian Press, Inc., West Hartford, CT, U.S.*

The Corporate Mystic, by Gay Hendricks, **Ph.D and Kate Ludeman, Ph.D,** *Bantam Books, New York,1996*

A Mythic Life, by **Jean Houston,** *1996, HarperSanFrancisco*

A Passion for the Possible, A Guide to Realizing Your True Potential, by **Jean Houston,** *1997, HarperCollins Publisher, San Francisco*

101 Best Home Based Businesses for Women, by **Priscilla Y. Huff,** *1995, Prima Publishing, U.S.*

Girls and Young Women Entrepreneurs, True Stories About Starting and Running a Business, by **Frances A. Karnes, Ph.D, and Suzanne M. Bean, Ph.D,** *1997 Free Spirit Publishing, U.S.*

Getting Down To Business, A Manual for Training Businesswomen, by **Uschi Kraus-Harper and Malcolm Harper,** *1992, Intermediate Technology Publications, London*

Woman To Woman, Street Smarts for Women Entrepreneurs, by **Geraldine A. Larkin,** *1993, Prentice Hall, New Jersey*

Working Solo Sourcebook, Second Edition, by **Terri Lonier,** *1995, 1998, John Wiley & Sons, Inc., New York*

The Small Business Money Guide, How to Get It, Use It, Keep It, by **Terri Lonier and Lisa M. Aldisert,** *1999, John Wiley& Sons, Inc., U.S.*

Hers, The Wise Women's Guide to Starting a Business On $2000 or Less, by **Carol Milano,** *1997, 1991, Allworth Press, New York*

Magical Gardens, Myth, Mulch and Marigolds, by **Patricia Monaghan,** *1997, Llewellyn Publications, US*

Cultivating Sacred Space, Gardening for the Soul, by **Elizabeth Murray,** *1997, Pomegranate, California*

Women's Bodies Women's Wisdom, by **Christiane Northrup,** *1998, 1994, Bantam Books, New York*

The 9 Steps to Financial Freedom, Practical and Spiritual Steps So You Can Stop Worrying, by **Suze Orman,** *1997, Crown Publishers, New York*

The Popcorn Report, Faith Popcorn on The Future of Your Company, Your World, Your Life, by **Faith Popcorn,** *1991, HarperBusiness, New York*

Organic Gardening, Your Seasonal Companion, by **Maria Rodale,** *1998, Rodale Press, Pennsylvania, U.S.*

Maps to Ecstacy, teaching of a urban shaman, by **Gabrielle Roth with John Loudon,** *1989, Nataraj Publishing, Mill Valley, CA*

Sweat Your Prayers, Movement as Spiritual Practice, by **Gabrielle Roth,** *1997, Jeremy P. Tarcher/Putnam, New York*

Succulent Wild Woman, Dancing With Your Wonder-full Self, by **Sark,** *1997, Fireside, New York*

The Bodacious Book of Succulence, by **Sark,** *1998, Fireside, New York*

Negotiating For Your Life: News Success Strategies For Women, by **Nicole Schapiro,** *1993, Henry Holt & Co.*

The Fifth Discipline, The Art and Practice of the Learning Organization, by **Peter M. Senge,** *1990, Doubleday, New York*

Leadership and the New Science, by **Margaret J. Wheatley,** *1992, Berret-Koehler Publishers, San Francisco*

ReWiring the Corporate Brain, Using the New Science to Rethink How We Structure and Lead Organizations, by **Danah Zohar,** *Berret-Koehler Publishers, Inc., San Francisco, CA*

Seed Contacts

INTERNATIONAL

Business and Professional Women International
Studio 16, Cloisters Business Centre
8 Battersea Park Road, London SW8 4BG England
Tel: 44(171) 738-8323 Fax: 44(171) 622-8528
www.bpwintl.com email: *bpwihq@cs.com*

Center for International Private Enterprise (CIPE)
1155 15th Street, NW, Suite 700, Washington, DC 20005
Tel: (202) 721-9200 Fax: (202) 721-9250
www.cipe.org/prog/women email: *cipe@cipe.org*
CIPE IS AN AFFILIATE OF THE US CHAMBER OF COMMERCE.

Les Femmes Chefs d'Enterprises Mondial (FCEM)
The World Association of Women Entrepreneurs
Leyla Khaiat, FCEM President
17, Rue Abderrahman el Jaziri,1002 Tunis Belvedere Tunisia
Tel: (216) 179-3432 Fax: (202) 721-9250
email: *plastiss@planet.tn*

Arline Woutersz, FCEM Vice President
114 Gloucester Place, London WIH 3DB UK
Tel/Fax: (171) 935-0085
email: *woutersz@msn.com*

Phyllis Hill Slater, FCEM Vice President
45 North Station Plaza, Suite L/100, Great Neck,
NY 11021 USA
Tel: (516) 773.7779 Fax: (516) 773.7729
email:*hillslater@aol.com*

ASIA

www.womenasia.com
Rosemary Brisco
76 Cape Hatteras Court
Redwood City, CA USA 94065
Tel: (650) 654-6926 Fax: (650) 654-6927
email: *info@womenasia.com*

THEY ARE A BUSINESS TO BUSINESS NETWORK CONNECTING
WOMEN IN ASIA AND NORTH AMERICA FOR THE PURPOSE OF
TRADE AND COMMERCE.

AUSTRALIA

Australian Federation of Business and Professional Women
PO Box 1267 Swan Hill, VIC 3585 Australia
Tel/Fax: (035) 032-0068
www.bpw.com.au email: *bpwaust@bpw.com.au*

BPW AUSTRALIA CO-OPERATES WITH BUSINESS AND
PROFESSIONAL WOMEN IN OTHER COUNTRIES TO ENCOURAGE
INTERNATIONAL UNDERSTANDING AND PROVIDES A FORUM FOR
THE DISCUSSIONS OF INTERNATIONAL, NATIONAL, STATE, AND
LOCAL ISSUES

CANADA

Canadian Women's Business Network
3995 MacIsaac Drive Nanaimo, B.C.
Canada V9T-3V5
Tel: 250.741.0947
www.cdnbiz.women.com

MEXICO

Del Verbo Emprender
Salo Grabinsky
Fuente de Piramides 20 P.B. Local B
Tecamachalco, Edo. De Mexico 539350 Mexico
(525) 294-8407
www.internet.com.nx/empresas/emprender

AL SERVICIO DE LOS EMPRENDADORES Y LA EMPRESA FAMILIAR.
HELPING LATIN AMERICAN AND HISPANIC ENTREPRENEURS.

220.

UNITED KINGDOM

Council on Economic Priorities (CEP)
38 Ebury Street, London SW1WOLU
Tel: 44(171) 730-2646 Fax: 44(171) 730-2664

www.cepaa.org

THE COUNCIL ON ECONOMIC PRIORITIES' MISSION IS TO
PROVIDE ACCURATE AND IMPARTIAL ANALYSIS OF CORPORATE
SOCIAL AND ENVIRONMENTAL PERFORMANCE AND TO PROMOTE
EXCELLENCE IN CORPORATE CITIZENSHIP. FOUNDED IN 1969.

European Federation of Black Women Business Owners
Suite One, Two Tunstall Rd., London SW9 8DA
Tel: 44(171) 978 9488 Fax: 44(171) 978 9490

www.blacknet.co.uk/womeninbusiness

email: asapcoms@dircon.co.uk

Social Venture Network (Europe)
4, Great James Street
London WC1N 3DA
Tel: (171) 881-9007 Fax: (171) 881-9008

www.svneurope.org

SOCIAL VENTURE NETWORK IS AN ASSOCIATION OF COMPANIES
AND INDIVIDUAL BUSINESS LEADERS WHO BELIEVE THEY CAN-
AND MUST-MAKE A SIGNIFICANT CONTRIBUTION TO SOLVE
SOCIAL AND ENVIRONMENTAL PROBLEMS LOCALLY AND GLOBALLY.

Network for Successful UK Women
94A Holland Road, Willesden, London NW10 5AY
Tel: (181) 963-1481 Fax: (181) 961-7468

www.networkwomenuk.org

email: netwomen@enterprise.net

The British Association of Women Entrepreneurs (BAWE)
Arline Woutersz, President
114 Gloucester Place
London WIH 3DB UK
Tel/Fax: (171) 935-0085

email: woutersz@msn.com

UNITED STATES

American Business Women's Association
9100 Ward Parkway, Kansas City, MO 64114-0728
Tel: (816) 361-6621 Fax: (816) 361-4991

www.abwaahq.org email: abwa@abwahq.org

BRINGING TOGETHER BUSINESS WOMEN OF DIVERSE OCCUPATIONS
AND PROVIDING OPPORTUNITIES FOR THEM TO HELP THEM-
SELVES AND OTHERS GROW PERSONALLY AND PROFESSIONALLY
THROUGH LEADERSHIP, EDUCATION, NETWORKING SUPPORT
AND NATIONAL RECOGNITION.

Business for Social Responsibility (BSR)
609 Mission Street, 2nd Floor
San Francisco, CA 94105-3506 US
Tel: (415) 537 0888 Fax: (415) 537-0889

www.bsr.org email: bsr@bsr.org

BSR'S MISSION IS TO BE A LEADING GLOBAL RESOURCE PROVIDING
MEMBERS WITH INNOVATIVE PRODUCTS AND SERVICES THAT
HELP COMPANIES BE COMMERCIALLY SUCCESSFUL IN WAYS
THAT DEMONSTRATE RESPECT FOR ETHICAL VALUES, PEOPLE,
COMMUNITY AND THE ENVIRONMENT.

Council on Economic Priorities (CEP)
30 Irving Place, New York, NY 10003
Tel: (212) 420-1133 Fax: (212) 420-0988

www.cepnyc.org

THE COUNCIL ON ECONOMIC PRIORITIES' MISSION IS TO
PROVIDE ACCURATE AND IMPARTIAL ANALYSIS OF CORPORATE
SOCIAL AND ENVIRONMENTAL PERFORMANCE AND TO PROMOTE
EXCELLENCE IN CORPORATE CITIZENSHIP. FOUNDED IN 1969.

Latin Business Association
5400 E. Olympic Blvd, Suite 130, LA, CA90022
Tel: 323 721-4000 Fax: 323.722.5050

www.lbausa.com

THE LBA IS A PROFESSIONAL ORGANIZATION DEDICATED TO THE
SUCCESS OF LATINO BUSINESSES WORLDWIDE.

National Association of Women Business Owners (NAWBO)
1100 Wayne Ave, Suite 830, Silver Spring,
MD 20910
Tel: (301) 608-2590 Fax: (301) 608-2596

www.nawbo.org email: national@nawbo.org

ACCESS INFORMATION ENABLING YOU TO BETTER UNDERSTAND
THE CURRENT STATE OF THE ECONOMY, TRENDS IN Y OUR
INDUSTRY, ADVANCES IN TECHNOLOGY, AND LEGISLATION
AFFECTING YOUR BUSINESS.

The National Black Business Trade Association (NBBTA)
P.O. Box 75022, Washington, DC 20013
Tel: (202)371-1000 Fax: (561) 673-0879

www.nbbta.org

THE NATIONAL BLACK BUSINESS TRADE ASSOCIATION (NBBTA), ESTABLISHED IN 1993 AS A NON-PROFIT ORGANIZATION, WAS CREATED TO SUPPORT, ENCOURAGE AND INSPIRE ENTREPRENEURSHIP IN THE AFRICAN AMERICAN COMMUNITY

National Foundation for Women Business Owners (NFWBO)
1100 Wayne Ave. Suite 830 Silver Spring, MD 20910-5603
Tel: (301) 495-4975 Fax: (301) 495-4979

www.nfwbo.org

EMAIL: NFWBO@WORLDNET.ATT.NETACCESS INFORMATION ENABLING YOU TO BETTER UNDERSTAND THE CURRENT STATE OF THE ECONOMY, TRENDS IN YOUR INDUSTRY, ADVANCES IN TECHNOLOGY, AND LEGISLATION AFFECTING YOUR BUSINESS.

Social Venture Network (US)
PO Box 29221 San Francisco, CA 94129-0221
Tel: (415) 561-6501 Fax: (415) 561-6435

www.svn.org email: svn@wenet.net

SOCIAL VENTURE NETWORK IS A NON PROFIT MEMBER-SHIP ORGANIZATION OF BUSINESSES AND SOCIAL ENTREPRENEURS DEDICATED TO CREATING A MORE JUST HUMANE AND SUSTAINABLE SOCIETY BY CHANGING THE WAY THE WORLD DOES BUSINESS.

The Womens Resource Directory
PO Box 66796, Houston, Texas 77266
Tel: (281) 242-0908

www.ghgcorp.com/worldweb

AN ENTREPRENEURS RESOURCE.

Women's Enterprise Development Corp.
100 W. Broadway, Suite 500, Long Beach, CA 90802
562 983 3747 Fax: 562.983.3750

www.wedc1.org email:wedc1@aol.com

PROVIDES BUSINESS ENTREPRENEURIAL MANAGEMENT TRAINING

Women in Business
Po Box 265 Palos Verdes Estates 90274
Tel: (310) 791-0113 Fax: 310.375.4208

www.wibla.org email: wibnews@aol.com

WOMEN IN BUSINESS IS A DIVERSE ORGANIZATION THAT PROVIDES LEADERSHIP TO EXPAND THE ROLE AND IMPACT OF WOMEN IN BUSINESS AND THE COMMUNITY. OUR PURPOSE IS TO PROMOTE THE PROFESSIONAL AND PERSONAL DEVELOPMENT, GROWTH AND VISIBILITY OF WOMEN.

Women Incorporated
333 South Grand Ave., Suite 2450
Los Angeles, CA 90071
800 930 3993 Fax: 213.680.3475

www.womeninc.com email: womeninc@aol.com

A NATIONAL MEMBERSHIP ORGANIZATION FOR BUSINESS OWNERS AND PROFESSIONALS TO GAIN ACCESS TO LOANS AND LINES OF CREDIT, HEALTH INSURANCE, AND BUSINESS DISCOUNTS AND SERVICES.

USEFUL WOMEN'S WEBSITES

Advancing Women

www.advancingwomen.com

INTERNATIONAL BUSINESS & CAREER COMMUNITY. NEWS, NETWORKING & STRATEGY FOR WOMEN

ChannelHealth.com

www.channelhealth.com

EVERTHING YOU NEED TO KNOW ABOUT YOUR BODY

Handbag.com

www.handbag.com

A WOMEN'S WEBSITE MAGAZINE WITH EVERYTHING FROM RELATIONSHIPS TO HEALTH, FASHION TO FINANCE

Independent Means
126 Powers Ave., Santa Barbara, CA 93103
Tel: (800) 350-1816

www.independentmeans.com

A RESOURCE AND SUPPORT WEBSITE FOR YOUNG WOMEN ENTREPRENEURS

iVillage.com

www.ivillage.com

WITHIN IVILLAGE.COM, THERE IS A COMMUNITY FOR EVERY INTEREST, AND LINKS TO MORE THAN 50 EXPERTS, THOUSANDS OF MESSAGE BOARDS, AND CONSTANT ACCESS TO A VOLUNTEER NETWORK OF 1,000+ "COMMUNITY LEADERS".

Online Women's Business Center
Tel: (800) 827 5722

www.onlinewbc.org

AN INFORMATION & RESOURCE CENTER CREATED IN TANDEM WITH THE US SMALL BUSINESS ADMINISTRATION

Small Business Administration

www.sba.gov

THE SMALL BUSINESS ADMINISTRATION IS RICH WITH INFORMATION ON HOW TO START YOUR BUSINESS AND HAS OFFICES IN PRACTICALLY EVERY STATE IN THE US. GO TO THIS WEBSITE TO LEARN WHICH ONES ARE CLOSEST TO YOU AND SO MUCH MORE. GO TO ONLINE WOMEN'S BUSINESS CENTER FOR MORE INFO.

women.com

www.Women.com

WITH THE COMBINED STRENGTH OF WOMEN.COM, HOMEARTS, ASTRONET, AND HEARST'S PORTFOLIO OF WOMEN'S MAGAZINE SITES, WOMEN.COM NETWORKS HAS THE LARGEST BREADTH OF RESOURCES OF ANY ONLINE WOMEN'S NETWORK.

wwwomen.com

www.wwwomen.com

THE MOST INCLUSIVE UP-TO-DATE SEARCH SITE FOR WOMEN'S TOPICS. THEIR TEAM OF ONLINE SURFERS HAVE COMPILED ONE OF THE MOST COMPREHENSIVE LISTS POSSIBLE.

LYNNE FRANKS founded her first company when she was twenty-one. After twenty highly successful years she sold her firm to focus on using her communications skills to encourage partnership between business and society. Leaving her London-based agency in 1992, Franks traveled the world interacting with multinationals, nation states, NGOs, and grass roots organizations.

She created the event "What Women Want" to draw attention to the changing position of women in society, prior to attending the Beijing women's conference; she chaired the UK's first women's radio station and has become a spokesperson on women's issues and socially responsible business practices.

Lynne Franks is currently developing SEED–Sustainable Enterprise Empowerment Dynamics, a network aimed at training and empowering, particularly with regard to sustainable enterprise. She is also founder of Globalfusion, a communications consultancy organization dedicated to making a positive difference in society through "new marketing" – connecting people, ideas, businesses, and development. She divides her time between California, the UK, and Spain.

ANN FIELD'S award-winning collages and bright illustrations are universally recognized to inspire. Her clients include Levi's Jeans for women, Hard Rock Hotel, and Barneys New York. She lives in Southern California.